# THE OKOBOJI KID

**Doug Andersen**
**1957**

## *Coming of age is tough, stuttering made it double-tough*

# ACKNOWLEDGMENT

*To Janice, who kept telling me for twenty-five years to "Just get it down on paper."*

## My Attempt at a Disclaimer:

Athough Ashton is a real town in Iowa, it is not the actual town I describe in the first chapter.

Except for my immediate and extended family members, most names have been changed. This was difficult to do since I have vivid memories associated with all the real names. They probably wouldn't have minded, but you never know.

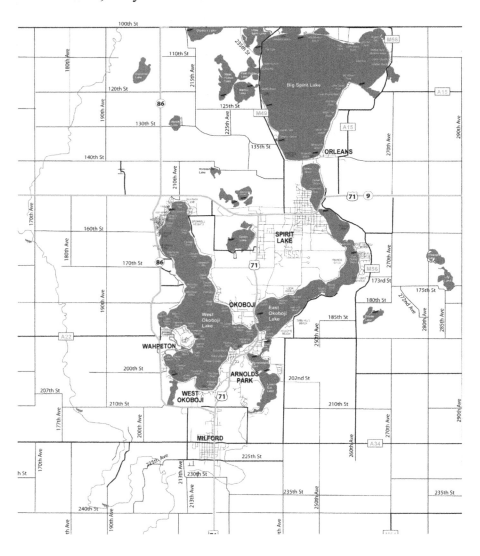

# TABLE OF CONTENTS

# CHAPTER ONE

# TURKEYS AND WATERMELON

Iowa is hot in the summer, and I swear it was hotter in the fifties. I'm talking small town hot. These were towns without even an air-conditioned movie house in which to hide from the inferno.

We lived in such an Iowa town, Spirit Lake, with a population somewhere around 2500 in the winter. In the summer, due to vacation homes, motels, and resorts on the many lakes and tourists wanting to get out of the cities and off the farms, that number would soar to 40,000.

Spirit Lake is situated in the northwest part of the state, about five miles south of the Minnesota border. Apparently, we got the tail end of Minnesota's 10,000 lakes, so at least we had a refuge from the afternoon furnace, unlike most farm towns dotted across Iowa.

Big Spirit Lake, and more notably, East and West Okoboji Lakes, are the three prominent bodies of water that get most of the attention. Due to the popularity of the latter two, and maybe due to the unusual name, the whole area is commonly referred to as just Okoboji (OH-KOE-BOE-GEE).

It's a dandy place to grow up. There's so much for a kid to do; one with imagination and time on his hands. The area had a rural atmosphere without having to survive on a farm tucked away on some backroad. The many lakes, ponds, sloughs, and woods that sprinkle the area were mostly within walking distances and were all ready to explore with a best friend and a dog. Burr oaks lined all the lake shores, giving the area its great beauty and visitor drawing factor. Fishing poles and peanut butter sandwiches were optional, but pretty much guaranteed a day of adventure.

Fishing, hunting, sailing, and water sports of all kinds were endlessly touted by the Chamber of Commerce to entice the surrounding out-of-staters to come join in on all the fun. There were many resorts, lodgings of various kinds, and campgrounds everywhere to fit every budget; at least so said the brochures. There's no Iowan above the age of fifteen who doesn't know of Okoboji.

In the off-season, however, Okoboji, for all practical purposes, shuts down for a long winter's nap. The locals ice fished and hunted pheasants and ducks, but mostly just waited for spring to arrive. It was always a long wait. Attending school in this tiny community made the waiting bearable for the kids. Life in wintry Iowa without school would have been cruel and unusual punishment. Still, I can't imagine growing up anywhere but Okoboji.

During the summer, my parents would sometimes send me packing to stay with friends or cousins in other little towns in the area, away from my beloved Okoboji. One particular time it was Ashton, a tiny community of only 500 Dutch-Reformed Lutherans, about sixty miles west of my home.

As with most little towns in Iowa, not necessarily Okoboji, Ashton revolved around farming. As farming went, the town went. I always found it interesting that farmers could gather in the town café and talk about their corn and bean crops for hours on end. They did this every day, most of them sporting John Deere caps and engineer bib overalls. The caps were, at one time, green and yellow, but over time they became the color of whatever axle grease is.

They ate their bacon and eggs and drank bottomless cups of coffee out of thick ivory colored cups, stained from years of use, served by someone named Shirley or Olive. Cigarette smoke was always hanging heavy in the air, giving the room a rather bluish hue. The linoleum tile floors were tracked with black Iowa mud when it rained and traces of it when it didn't. Hank Williams, Eddy Arnold, and Jim Reeves usually hogged all the quarters in the jukebox. Sometimes a few of the wives would join their husbands in the booths, but it was routinely frowned upon.

In the summer, the conversation revolved around the current crop in the ground. The fall season would bring topics of crop prices and how they're all getting screwed by government programs that paid them to leave some of their lands fallow. Winter brought stories of broken equipment and the local high school football team's lousy coach. Of course, the coach might be in the booth behind them, so a lowered voice was always the smart move. In the spring, it started all over again, beginning with complaints of the inflated costs of some new combine or tractor someone had his eye on. This was also the time the merits of one seed corn company over the others were hotly debated. The farmers all looked poor as church mice and drove pickups to match the disguise.

---

To illustrate this point, let me interject something: Not too long ago, my father sent me a recent picture of himself and three of his old high school buddies, all of them in their late eighties. They were the lone survivors of their entire high school class of nine, also the only boys in the class. The five women had all passed away. He noted that all three of his old friends, all farmers, were now millionaires. Dad was the only non-farmer, the only veteran, and, unfortunately, the only non-millionaire in the group.

---

So, back to Ashton: There I was, staying with Ron Barker, one of the sons of Randal and Pearl, who operated a huge turkey farm about 5 miles outside of town. They chose to live in town probably to be as far away from the smelly birds as possible.

As I stated earlier, Iowa has a heat all its own. Living in Phoenix now, I'm more than familiar with what hot is, but Iowa can still take the misery index trophy from time to time, depending on the humidity.

On my first day there, Ron and I were chasing turkeys in the hot sun. Ron hated those huge white birds more than anyone should hate anything. He hated the way they looked. He hated the way they smelled. He hated the way they gobbled, but most of all, he hated their stupidity.

His dad would cut off the top of the turkey's beak about half way back so they wouldn't peck each other to death. However, as a result of this procedure, they are susceptible to drowning. Apparently the beak-altered birds would look up in the heavens to investigate what was falling on them from above, allowing the rain to fill their lungs. It never rained while I was out there, so I never got to see that happen. I always wanted to, though.

Ron was a tall kid, getting his height from both parents. He was pleasant to be around except when the subject turned to turkeys which, not surprisingly, it did quite often. His head was shaped somewhat like an owl's. When I mentioned that to him, he said he was just glad it wasn't shaped like a turkey head. He introduced me to the world of Buddy Holly while I was visiting. He knew all the words to *Peggy Sue* and could do a fairly good rendition of it.

In the summer, it didn't get dark until around ten o'clock, so we ate later than usual. Dinner was an outdoor event since air conditioning was still a pipe dream. Corn on the cob, hot dogs, and hamburgers were normally on the menu, and for dessert, there was always watermelon.

Crisp, cold, watermelon. Crisp, cold, sweet, juicy, watermelon.

I had been looking forward to this stuff all day while playing in the heat, so I was ready to feast. The best thing about eating watermelon outside is that no one expects to look good doing it. It was just a matter of grabbing a big wedge, starting in the center to avoid the seeds, and working my way down the good part. Of course, the deeper I ate, the better the chance of ending up with seeds in my ears.

Eating the seeded part of the melon required a little more work due to the spitting process. Many ways have been invented to bother melon eating friends when it came to the fine art of seed-spitting. It goes with the territory. However, this night it was just about eating as much of it as I could before it was gone.

When I was finished, I thumped my belly, and it made the same sound as the melon did before we cut into it. I'd had a full day of turkey chasing and watermelon eating, and now I was dog tired. We didn't argue when Ron's mother mentioned it was time for bed. There I was, a chronic bed wetter, sleeping in a double bed with my friend Ron and loaded with watermelon.

What could go wrong?

It happened about four in the morning. It always did. Adolescent sleep is almost like being dead. Most bed-wetters don't just open up the floodgates unknowingly. It doesn't work that way. Decisions have to be made before it happens. The perpetrators usually run through a checklist while dreaming. I always knew what I was doing. The problem was I was unconscious at the time. There wasn't one time I woke up surprised that I had wet myself. My dreams had always convinced me that it was safe to go. That was the cruel twist in this dilemma.

---

Let me attempt to clarify this process: I had a system of checkpoints while dreaming to help prevent the terrible outcome. This system was supposed to lead me to the conclusion that I was not awake, and thus, not to trust my final decisions. Unfortunately, they just added to the validity of the ruse. My supposed fail-safe system was not up to the task of convincing me that I was actually asleep in a warm, dry bed.

In my dream world, I was always safely sitting on a toilet somewhere. I might be on the top of the Arc de Triomphe with a French-speaking crow reassuring me it was perfectly fine to relieve myself. I'd look around and assess the entire situation, reexamine everything with great care to make sure I wasn't being fooled again.

The checklist with all the relevant facts and correlating evidence concerning the decision whether or not to let 'er fly would look something like this:

1) Immediate situation: Sitting on a toilet. Check.
2) Toilet location: Paris, France. Check.
3) Large audience: Of course. Check.
4) Reason for being there: Saving beautiful girl trapped on top of the tower. Check.
5) Any doubts as to the legitimacy of this situation? You bet.

No matter how ridiculous the situation was in my dreams, I couldn't persuade myself that I was being duped; that I might want to hold it for further review.

Sometimes my dreams would add the element of flying in the adventure. After all, I needed to get to the damsel in distress on top of the tower. Elevators in dreams never worked. At least mine didn't.

Flying always took a great deal of work. I'm not sure if the advantages of it ever outweighed the effort. As a matter of fact, I was pretty much grounded as I grew into young adulthood. Thus, I would have to resort to running up sandy mountains to escape from the bad guys like everyone else did; but for now, I could fly.

It was quite a pleasant sensation, especially if I could elevate myself high enough to shift into a glide mode. This would let me enjoy the ride without having to exert so much energy. Gliding over the tops of trees and buildings was exhilarating, but always short in duration.

Before my dramatic liftoff heavenward, I'd think, why not relieve myself before I go? After all, I was sitting on a toilet in a perfectly safe and logical place. There's certainly nothing unusual about sitting on a toilet on top of the Arc de Triomphe surrounded by tourists. My checklist had more than validated my situation with room to spare.

It was at this time that the nagging lingering doubt on the bottom of my list was beginning to annoy me. It was suggesting that I re-think this decision to relax my sphincter; that something wasn't quite as it seemed. However, I never could overrule my dream world.

---

So, soundly slumbering in Ron's bed, on this particular night, everything had been cleared to my satisfaction. Apparently, it was perfectly safe to proceed with the process of the great unloading. Everything was A-OK. It was a go.

And go I did. I unloaded my personal Lake Okoboji all over my friend Ron.

In the past, there were many times I stopped myself partway through a soaking by emerging out of my slumber. Tonight, waking a hibernating grizzly would have been easier. After chasing turkeys all day in the hot sun, it was not going to happen. At least not until I was drained. That's when I immediately awoke and, to my horror, realized I had been fooled again, big time. Rats!

I pulled back my part of the covers to inspect the damage.

Again, rats!

Heavy blankets, not a good sign. Wait, maybe it was just on my side of the bed! Maybe if I lift my covers and prop them up with something, everything might dry before anyone is the wiser.

Gently touching around Ron, I discovered that his side was even more soaked than mine.

Crap!

His side was so drenched, in fact, that his pajamas were wet all the way up his back.

I was doomed. There was no way out of this one. I was trapped like a coon in a tree. I was screwed. Ron would be a prune in the morning. A urine-soaked stinking prune.

What could I do? I couldn't just roll over and pretend it didn't happen. Maybe I could blame Ron. No, a phone call to my mom would nix that plan. Besides, the front side of his pajamas was probably dry.

I couldn't face him when he woke up. I had to come up with something good. I had to logically assess the entire situation and come up with the best possible plan to help me out this mess.

What were my assets? I was ten; I had no assets. In my way of thinking I only had two viable options:
1) Stay there and be humiliated and probably beaten up, or
2) Run like hell.
I chose the latter.

The first thing I needed to do was to get out of these bed clothes … these stinking, wet bed clothes.

Since it was still dark, I silently gathered all my stuff in my little suitcase and went into the only bathroom in the house so I could dress in the light. It was located on the second floor along with all the bedrooms. I could clean up there a bit; pack my suitcase, and skee-dattle.

Walking into the rather large tile bathroom, I glared at the toilet, giving it the evil eye. Having absolutely no need for its services at the moment, I started my packing routine thinking I was quite safe from intrusion at this hour of the day. After all, who gets up at four in the morning?

Let me tell you who gets up at four in the morning … turkey farmers.

I heard Ron's parents' door open down the hallway. Randal, Ron's dad, was coming to join me in the bathroom in all my ruin. Even at this ungodly hour I couldn't manage to make a clean getaway.

Panic mode settled in. I knew I could never successfully explain to this rather tall man what I was doing up at this hour packing my suitcase with soaked shorts.

Not only was I a prolific bed-wetter, but being a stutterer as well, I could only imagine what scenario was about to unfold. Randal was about to witness a frightened, embarrassed little boy standing in the bathroom in wet shorts, suitcase opened and his soaked pajamas lying on the tile floor. How was I ever going to explain in my tortured language what, in the name of Moses, I was doing there at this early hour?

This simply was not going to happen. The only thing I could do was turn off the light, pull the door open to leave a small wedge of space for me to hide behind, and hope for the best. After all, this sort of thing always seemed to work in cartoons, Westerns, and with the *Three Stooges*.

Of course, if he closed the door after turning on the light, I was a dead duck.

Randal came in, turned on the light and went straight to the commode. He stood over it for what was the longest time, leaning on the facing wall with his left arm for support. It seemed to be never ending until the several obligatory short squirts at the end. He then began what was, I assume, his morning ritual of grunts, coughs, hacks, scratches, and flatulent exercises.

I wondered if this was what all grown men do. I never saw my dad do it. How do wives overlook this stuff and stay married to these Neanderthals? Women would never display such poor practices when alone in their powder rooms, I thought to myself.

He turned off the light and walked down the stairs.

Maybe he knew I was there, and he just didn't want to deal with the weird kid standing behind the door.

Be that as it may, I thought I had just pulled off a major victory in my great escape. Now I could go on with my planned departure.

I changed into dry clothes, hurriedly packed my things, and sneaked down the stairs. I waited until he drove away before slipping out the back door.

I walked a couple blocks to what was Ashton's downtown. It consisted of a farm implement place and a few other businesses. The obligatory café was located on the outskirts of town. I imagined the bean and corn stories were in full throttle by now. Randal would be there, too, talking turkey.

Not too surprisingly, the street was deserted. The air was still and fresh and moist, but warming up. Alfalfa had been cut and baled recently and left its familiar sweet scent to pervade throughout the area. A couple of dogs were barking in the distance, and there was the familiar sound of a pickup truck shifting gears, but other than that, it was stone cold quiet. I was alone with all my troubles, doubts, fears, and humiliations and a suitcase full of wet pissy clothes.

I found what amounted to be the town square or city park. It was, in fact, a horseshoe tossing pit consisting of two stakes, some sand, and the metal shoes situated between two old buildings. All four of the shoes were there. No one in town would steal them. Why would they? Even if they did, every citizen would know who did in a matter of three days. Everyone knew everything about everybody, which was one more reason I had to "get out of Dodge." My whizzing on Randal's oldest boy would become a hot topic for the good old boys in the café in an hour. A story like that would take precedence over beans and corn.

I put my suitcase down and tossed the iron footwear, wondering how I was going to ever get back home. After a long while and a couple of ringers, my interest in the tossing game began to wane. The sun was officially up now and heating the air at an alarming rate. I dropped the horseshoes, picked up my stuff, and walked to the edge of town, not knowing if the road before me even led to Okoboji.

Exhaustion was setting in due to my four-in-the-morning wake-up call. The temperature was getting uncomfortable now, and I was also becoming hungry. Ron's mother, Pearl, would be making pancakes and bacon, and that thought was eroding my desire to flee.

Flee to where? Where could I go? I was sixty miles from Okoboji, but it may as well been a million.

I had no idea where home was or how to get there. I came to realize that I had no more options. I had to go back to the scene of the unspeakable crime.

I walked back slowly, unconvinced I was making the right move, but the thought of breakfast kept me on target. When I got to the back door, I could smell bacon in the air.

If only I could be someone else for a while instead of the stutter-box kid who drenched Ron. I didn't want to pee on Ron. I had no desire to pee on anyone. Why did this stuff always happen to me? Why did I always have to be the DDK, the Designated Disaster Kid?

Notwithstanding, I had to go in and face the music, so I opened the door. The long spring on the screen door announced my arrival with the familiar twang sound of steel coils on worn wood. I was the prodigal son looking for forgiveness and pancakes.

Hunger, exhaustion, and humiliation are a strange combination to endure at the age of ten. The two younger siblings at the table turned and looked at me dead-on in complete silence. Ron wouldn't even look up. His head stayed face-down in his plate. He was smoldering.

Pearl, who was passing out pancakes, looked at me and said, "Don't worry, Honey, it happens sometimes. Here, have some pancakes, Sweetie."

Even though she may have meant it, I could tell she was as disgusted as Ron. She had lost a good mattress, and now she had extra laundry to do.

I sat at the table, too embarrassed to look up. Pearl served my pancakes and bacon. Any attempt at small talk wasn't in the cards. We all sat there in silence and ate our breakfast. I knew I was on my way home somehow and was relieved by the thought. Ben Franklin's old adage "Fish and visitors smell in three days," was accomplished way ahead of schedule.

Pearl's attempt at being kind and forgiving helped me feel better, or at least the pancakes did. I knew that the comment "it happens sometimes," was a vain attempt to hide her underlying anger because, for sure, it had never happened in her house before.

Once she came to see us in Okoboji after this incident to show my parents her brand new black Cadillac. I was admiring it and innocently touched the chrome door handle, just to feel what new shiny chrome was like. She brushed my hand away and rubbed off the fingerprints. I had ruined her mattress, so don't dare touch my Cadillac. She was like that.

I was shuffled off back home later on that day in a meat delivery truck that Dad knew was making a trip to Okoboji, cutting my week stay short about five days.

Ron never talked to me again until twenty-five years later in a chance meeting at my brother's house in Phoenix. We talked about the old days in Iowa and how our families were doing and how we were doing. We never mentioned what surely was on both our minds.

# CHAPTER TWO

# DOUBLE WHAMMY

I remember getting up in the mornings and making a pledge that this was the time I wasn't going to stutter once all day.

It lasted about three minutes.

It's hard to say when I first noticed my speech disfluency or what profound effect it was going to have in shaping my life. Most therapists agree that around the age of five it sort of sets in if it's going to. Supposedly men are more susceptible than women. I've yet to know more than two women who stammered.

We stutterers can always spot others who were blessed with the same curse. We develop a keen sense of stutter-radar. It's tough to fool a fellow stammerer, no matter how well adapted they might have become or what tricks they may employ.

I was never too embarrassed about my problem until around the age of six. It was then I first noticed the obligatory phrases being directed at me; "stutter box," "tongue-tied," or "cat's got your tongue." I would excuse myself while watching cartoons with anyone other than my family whenever Porky Pig came on. Mel Blanc, the voice of Porky, was dead-on, but definitely not funny to me. Every stutter Porky made was a stake in my heart.

"Gee," some smart-ass kid would blurt out, "you talk just like him!"

I would be fuming, "Oh, d-d-do y-y-you think so, Sh-sh-sherlock?"

Of course, all the attention only made it worse. Not to say I didn't deserve it some of the time. The insults might be hurled after I called my sister a tub o' lard or fatso or any other number of nifty and original names.

It's not difficult to understand her mocking me after my cruel outburst with, "Oh y-y-ya? Y-y-you t-t-tub of l-l-lard!"

I had used my best barb, and it was turned entirely against me. Instead of her crying to Mom, she was laughing and repeating what I had just said, verbatim, accentuating each stammer. She hadn't a vengeful bone in her body, but kids will be kids. The "stones and glass houses" allegory was one I needed to learn; the quicker, the better.

My preschool speaking ability had yet to cause concern, at least for me. I wasn't fully aware anything was amiss. Even though I might be mocked at times, there was no lasting humiliation. The safety zone of home kept most of the hurtful barbs at bay. This was family. They all accepted me, laughed with me, played with me and apparently loved me. That acceptance would change when I started school.

When entering kindergarten, it became apparent I was not like all the other kids. There were one hundred students in my class, and I was the only one who stuttered. Some of them were amused by my different way of speaking, thus, making it more public than I'd known before. Suddenly realizing I was doing something wrong caused me to begin the process of masking the curse, which brought more attention to my affliction sometimes to the point of ridicule. I began to focus on my disability for the first time. I managed to get along well enough in most school activities and exercises without much hesitation or trouble until we started school's most important function. Learning to read.

I mastered the mechanics of reading well enough; I just didn't want to ever have to do it aloud in the classroom. There were countless times when everyone in the class would be asked to read a sentence or paragraph one at a time, seat by seat, row by row. I would freeze. I never heard what was being read by the others. I was only concerned about which part would be coming up for me to stumble through.

I'd do a quick count of the kids ahead of me, then inventory the sentences until I came up with what would be my part to read. I checked it out for any tough words. Usually, ones with strong consonants like gutter or purple or cluster would trigger a speech blockage. Anything beginning with the letters "b, d, g, j, k, l, m, n, p, q, r, s, t, v, w or y" would become glaring roadblocks. Or, in other words, pretty much the entire English language.

Embarrassment was ever present in the classroom for me. Mortification would be a better word for it.

When my turn finally came around to read, I would've already left for the bathroom.

I assumed at the time they all knew why I had disappeared, however, now as I look back, I don't believe one person in there had a clue as to the unending and constant turmoil I faced daily, hourly. Everyone owned a bag of demons to deal with while growing up and probably had no time to be bothered with mine. I see that now; I didn't then.

Sometimes I couldn't thwart an imposed reading in class. If the turns went alphabetically, with my name, I was usually first. I wouldn't have enough time to proof-read my part, so I had to just dive into it; or, in my case, belly flop.

If I faltered on the first word, I was doomed. My ears heated up and turned bright red; I couldn't hear anything from that moment on until the humiliation clock had run out. I wouldn't look up from my desk for a full fifteen minutes for fear of seeing laughing faces all around me, or worse, pity.

Fortunately, my problem didn't keep me away from acquiring friendships. I was, surprisingly, an outgoing kid and hung with the more popular crowd, if it's possible to have such a group in a small town in Iowa.

Once in fourth grade, a substitute lady teacher told me I was going to be a handsome young man someday. I was wearing a white turtleneck sweater. I wore it often after that. Actually, I wore it out.

Girls seemed to like me well enough, so life wasn't all misery. I remember being chased by Kimberly Wilson and Susie Phelps in kindergarten. I pretended to trip and fall so they could catch me, only to fend them off when they got too close. This was my first indication that I wasn't just someone's brother with yellow teeth and it was quite a thrill at the age of five. It also happened to coincide with my much improved dental hygiene regiment.

I saw Susie Phelps for the first time walking on the sidewalk near my home the summer before we started our life of school together. We lived a block away from each other. She was five years old and had the most gorgeous sun-bleached blonde hair. It was combed back in a ponytail which fell down to her waist. Susie brought me to the realization that little boys and little girls are somehow different. Sisters can't do that.

When kids turned five in small towns during the fifties they emerged from their houses and were allowed to venture beyond their property lines without parents nearby. I say that because I don't remember seeing her before then. This practice could be compared to bear cubs poking their heads out from their long winter's den for the first time in the spring, exposing themselves to their new world.

Wondering at that time if I was as cute as she was, in our bathroom, I grabbed a chair, climbed up, and took a gander. I'd never consciously looked at myself before. Studying my image, the face looking back at me could've been worse.

Growing up in a small town has its own set of unique advantages. One of those was having the same kids in class year after year as we advanced through school. We'd all known each other from the time we were five years old. The only people we'd known longer were our own families. Since this arrangement was all we knew, it wasn't different; it was normal.

In a way, our relationships with the opposite sex evolved into friendship varieties or even sibling ones, rather than romantic ones. This would eventually carry over into the dating age. I had only one date with one girl from my class during the entire high school run. These people were friends and confidants, not romantic prospects.

Besides, I'd seen half of them throw up their lunch when the flu was going around. Seeing the half-digested remains of goulash dribbling down a dress and onto the floor wasn't something easy to forget when contemplating a good-night kiss.

This isn't to say I didn't have adolescent crushes on several girls, sometimes even a few at the same time, before high school came around. Sometimes out of the blue I was told that someone I liked was announcing that she liked me back. These revelations were what kept the drudgery of those long school days in wintry Iowa worth waking up for; that and french toast.

The resulting elation would last a week or more. My way of dealing with this new and exciting development was to avoid seeing or talking to my new admirer at all costs. I didn't want her to stop liking me, and I reckoned that by actually talking to her using my sad version of conversation would probably kill the deal.

I'd see my newest admirer in the halls or at recess or after school with her friends and I'd wave and run. It had to be most confusing to them though making perfect sense to me. This rather strange mating ritual went on until I heard from the class matchmaker that she didn't like me anymore. A bit of sad news, but not unexpected, and now I wouldn't have to avoid her any longer. We could go back to just being friends as before.

There was one girl I did like more than most, probably from third grade on. Her name was Peggy Smart. Every school has one of these girls, someone who could do no wrong. The teachers adored her. She got straight-A's, sang soprano, danced, acted, played a variety of instruments, and, of course, was pretty.

She usually got to wear the queen crown on the day we played math flashcards. Phil Rettner or Larry Jacobsen got to wear the boy's king crown most of the time. The teacher had us line up in two lines of around fifteen kids each. The front two contestants competed for an opportunity to advance to the next round. The loser sat down, deflated. When my turn at the flash card came, I knew the answers, but couldn't spit them out fast enough. This is not to take anything away from Phil or Larry. Head on, they would have beaten my best anyway, but I was usually shot down in the first couple of waves.

One red-letter day in fifth grade I found out Peggy liked me. I immediately went into my cowardly wave and run mode, but I did buy her a silver heart necklace a week or so later and put it in her locker. She wore it that day, which made me immensely happy.

One day while walking home from school with friends I had to blow my nose. Since I was outside with my guy friends, and out of clean sleeves, there's only one way to accomplish that and keep pace with my buddies. I plugged a nostril and blasted out the slimed-filled one all over the sidewalk.

Unbeknownst to me, Peggy wasn't more than twenty feet behind us walking with her friend. I discovered they were there when I heard them squeal in disgust, "Oooh, yuck!" I turned around to find them stepping around my discarded goo.

"Well," I said matter-of-factly, "that ought to do it."

I found the necklace in my locker the next day.

I kept the silver locket in my drawer at home. All it did was remind me of that depressing day, so I ended up sending it to a girl from a distant town who I'd met at a church camp the next summer. Someone I hardly knew. When my mother found out what I was about to do, she told me not to waste such a thoughtful gift on someone I would never see again. She suggested instead that I give it to my sister, Marcia.

Being a romantic, I didn't see the rewards in such a move, so in the mail and off to Manning, Iowa it went. My sweet, loving, little sister would have loved a gift from her big brother. She deserved such a gift. Mom was right. What pleasures I would have received in return. I always wanted a do-over on that one.

A couple of years later someone told me Peggy liked me again. We never knew when revelations such as this were forthcoming, they just happened. At the time, it was customary for the boys to emblazon, in big bold letters, the name of their girlfriend on the binder of their three-ringed notebook; the one we usually carried around all day. Since I had no access to a felt-tipped marker, I had to rely on a black ballpoint pen instead, making the project tedious.

My notebook cover was made from a canvas-like blue cloth, which made it quite difficult to transfer ink onto its surface, especially anything bold. After finishing it, I was proudly showing it to one of Peggy's friends when she began laughing and pointed out that I had misspelled her name. I was mortified. I tried to erase it, then wash it. It turned into a big blob of black ink. I could have bought a new notebook and started over, but I figured she wouldn't like me long enough to make the investment worthwhile. Sometimes it was easier just being good friends.

I wish I could say that my speech problem was the only concern as a kid growing up, but I was dealt a double whammy. As I pointed out in the previous chapter, I was also a prolific bed-wetter. I've often wondered which came first; sort of the chicken or the egg quandary. All I needed was polio for strike three.

I had to live with the constant threat of soaking my bed and having to inform Mom she had more work to do that day than she had planned.

I'm not sure when my bed-wetting episodes began. Maybe they just continued from infancy. Mom would always remind me to go to the bathroom before I went to bed. Sometimes I did, sometimes not.

As usual, I'd wake up after unloading and realize my dreams had fooled me yet again into thinking I was sitting on a toilet somewhere. I had complete confidence that it was safe to go, so I would, only to be crushed to learn the truth moments after the event occurred. The familiar guilt and dreading would unfold over my groggy mind, then I'd fall back to sleep in my wet bed.

In the morning I'd stand at the top of the stairs and yell down, "Mom, I wet the bed again!"

She'd vent her frustration with, "Oh Doug, not again? Damn it!"

She wasn't one to curse, but I imagine this was getting tiresome. She'd take my sheets down to the basement and wash them in her old Maytag, drying them on a line strung down there in winter or outside in the summer. It wouldn't have been such a problem if I only wet my bed Sunday nights since wash day was always Monday. However, my bed-wetting was occurring on average two random nights a week.

Mike and I slept in the boy's room where we each had our own twin bed with cowboys and lassos embroidered on the bedspreads. I'm thinking the twin bed idea was pretty much his. Mom had resorted to covering my mattress with a waterproof fitted plastic sheet. This thing crackled whenever anyone even looked at it the wrong way, so whenever one of my friends would sit on it, they'd ask what was making that sound.

I explained the only way I could; I told them about the bed-wetter mattress protector and that they probably shouldn't be sitting on my brother's bed.

This was payback for the time Mike yelled downstairs to Mom, "He's wetting the bed again, and this time he's doing it from the hallway!"

Mom must have been searching for a solution to cure my bed-wetting. More than likely, most of her friends knew what was going on and were providing her with some sure cures. One day she announced a solution in which I was totally on board.

She had made a calendar chart and told me I'd be getting a star for every night I didn't have an accident, as the wetting incidents came to be known.

Now, I was thinking I was getting one of those shiny tin sheriff's badges that the Ben Franklin store was selling for ten cents. Whenever I wore one of those on my shirt, I felt like a sheriff; I was important. To have a badge given to me several times a week was quite an unexpected surprise.

I went to sleep that night with visions of hundreds of those stars covering my part of the wall in our room. After all, in a little while, there wouldn't be enough space on my shirt to pin them all.

Mom made good on her promise the next day since I didn't have an accident during the night. I waited with much anticipation as she pulled something out of the drawer. She handed me a tiny box with hundreds of red star cutouts jammed inside and told me to lick the back of one and stick it on the chart.

These were tiny stupid paper stars, not the shiny metal badges I'd been expecting. I tried to hide my disappointment, but it was just impossible. Not only did I feel cheated out of my sheriff's badges, but now my embarrassing tell-tale accident schedule was hung on the kitchen wall for everyone and his dog to see.

This stayed up there for a couple of weeks, long enough for me to have to explain to several friends what each star represented. Of course, the blank spaces represented something else, and my brother and sisters were having a jolly old time sharing that information with all their friends. Before long, everyone in town would know about me and my faulty sphincter.

I took the bed-wetting beacon down and burned it. It wasn't helping me anyway. Badges? I don't need no stinking badges.

**My mother, Hazel Lee Edelen and her mother, Myrle**
**Circa 1943**

# CHAPTER THREE

# THE BOY IN THE LIGHT BLUE DRESS

In first grade there was an unwritten new rule; any boy who fell in the mud on rainy days during recess had to wear a dress the rest of the day. We all knew the rule, but no one had ever seen the dress. Apparently, the principal had had his fill of kids not having sense enough during recess to keep clean and dry. He then had to call their moms to bring down another set of clothes every time a boy fell into the mud.

Iowa dirt is the blackest on the planet. Though farmers love it, it can't be worn around all day, nor easily brushed off. The stuff needs to be washed off, or it remains on floors, walls, and Levi-covered knees.

It seemed this rule only applied to the boys. On rainy days or warmer snowmelt days, all the girls would gather near the school doors, chew gum, and watch the boys make fools of themselves. The girls were wagering who might be the first unlucky cross-dresser.

We all hoped this warning was floated out there just to make us more careful, but we dreaded the thought of wearing a dress so much that we tried hard to remain vertical. Whenever someone landed on his knees, we saw him frantically scrubbing off the telltale dirt with puddle water or melting snow on the other side of the building, out of sight of the teachers.

One day it happened. Cole Cook, innocently enough, fell out of a swing and landed headfirst into the ever-present mud-filled furrow. When he pulled himself out of the muck, he had black Iowa slime covering his face and the entire front of his clothes. He was minstrel show material. Only the whites of his eyes were clean.

We all pointed and laughed uncontrollably, until the reality set in. Was the principal going to make good on his dress threat? Was he even allowed to do this terrible thing? Although it was a rather cold spring day and Cole was soaked to the gills with muddy water, we were certain poor Cole wasn't concerned about how chilled he was. He was shivering uncontrollably, and we all knew why; he was coming to terms with the new blue dress code.

The teacher immediately approached Cole, being careful not to get too close, grabbed his ear and they both walked into the building to face his impending doom. Nobody, but nobody wanted to be in his muddy shoes.

By the time recess ended everyone knew that some poor sap had fallen into the mud. Where was this unfortunate? Had he simply gone home to change? Was he in the principal's office waiting for his mother to show up with a fresh pile of clothes? Could they truly be so mean as to put poor Cole in a dress?

We were all gathered in the busy hallway making our way into our various classrooms, probably 200 kids in all, when Cole made his grand entrance. The principal had made good on his threat; there he was for all to see.

Cole was wearing a light blue dress with puffy sleeves and buttons down the front. The lower half of the dress extended out almost like a ballerina costume, cruelly exposing his skinny legs and still muddy shoes. His face was now clean and his eyes were wide open. He was in a suspended state of shock. We were all too horrified to make fun. All we could do was stare at this poor mortified creature. The only way it could have been worse was if the dress had been pink and his head adorned with a tiara.

The dress incident stayed fresh in our thoughts, but it didn't stop us boys from playing in the rain or the melting snow during recess; we just had to be careful and stay upright.

My turn came as sure as flies on a cow pie. I was on that same swing with the same mud hole under it where Cole had met his fate when someone pushed me and down I went. Immediately, all activity on the playground ceased. It was about to be Showtime again, and I had commandeered the starring role.

I'm not sure why Cole hadn't made a dash for home when he fell. I certainly thought about it. Maybe he couldn't bring himself to believe they'd actually do it. When the teacher grabbed me, I was doing my best to explain to anyone who'd listen that it wasn't my fault, that I had been shoved.

Inside the school, we went to find the janitor, the keeper of the light blue dress. Why did this stuff have to happen to me? With a hundred kids out there, why was it always me? This may turn out to be the worst day of my short life. I wasn't sure how Cole recovered from his transgendering, if he ever did, but I was about to find out what real embarrassment was all about.

We found the janitor down the hall. Judging from the smirk on his face, he had already guessed what was about to happen. The three of us walked to his maintenance room where the blue dress was hanging on a nail. I hadn't noticed while Cole was wearing it, but along the bottom, there was a white frilly ruffle. Maybe the old grump had his wife sew it on just for the likes of me. As if someone that mean and perverted could ever find anyone to marry him.

Good heavens! By this time, I was turning colors. Why couldn't this just be a bad dream? Cole was certainly never going to be the same again, and even though I had more experience with total humiliation, this may be too much for even me to absorb.

Outside the janitor's door were 200 kids waiting for me to make my entrance. All eyes were on the other side of that door, and I knew it.

Out of nowhere, a miracle unfolded. The skies opened up, the angels began singing, and sunshine fell all around me.

"Vern," Miss Nelson asked the man, "do you have a spare pair of overalls for Doug to wear? I have reason to believe it wasn't his fault." Old Vern reluctantly complied.

Did I hear this right? Was I going to be spared? Was I about to walk out that janitor's door and disappoint a couple of hundred kids? My relationship with her was going to be on a brand new level. I decided then and there to not cause a bit of trouble in her class again. Maybe my luck was beginning to take a turn for the better.

———

Let me illustrate the impact of this story: At our high school's twentieth-year graduation reunion, I was asked to address the class using a silly list someone had made during the last week of high school. It was a list prognosticating what everyone would be doing in twenty years. I was providing my best comedic spin on what was truly pitiful material. As I read down the list, there were chuckles here and there and other polite responses, as a few in the crowd would recall what some of the incidences were about that had inspired a particular entry. When Cole's name came up, I paused, mentioning that I didn't think he was in the packed audience and believed I knew why.

Putting down my notes and looking straight at them I asked, "Do any of you remember poor Cole in that light blue dress?"

An immediate explosion of laughter shook the meeting room. I couldn't go on with my presentation for at least ten minutes. My former classmates were blowing drinks through their noses. All it took was one simple question to bring back the vivid memory forever seared in their brains.

We would never forget the sight of that little boy with skinny legs in a light blue dress standing in the middle of 200 kids in the hall, his eyes filled with terror.

---

The following story will explain how a few years can change a kid's outlook on what's humiliating and what's exhilarating.

It was fourth grade, and I was in the usual Peggy-liking mode again. I knew she was staying for the evening with her good friend Rhonda Swift; who lived about three or four blocks from me on the only busy street in Spirit Lake.

I had never had any meaningful conversation with Peggy because I couldn't bring myself to talk to her. No ten-year-old boy knows how to carry on a conversation with girls. Especially someone he likes a lot. Even if I had known the secrets of what to say, I would never have been able to get through any sentence without facial distortions and word repetitions. I could never put her through that, or myself.

An idea was forming. If I couldn't be me and talk to her, maybe I could be someone else and give it a shot. For some inexplicable reason, I decided to dress up as a woman and pay the girls a surprise visit.

Our home was an old two story with a full, creepy basement and a creepier attic. In the attic, along with a vast assortment of other stuff, my mother's discarded clothes were all hanging on a long pole. There were lots of dresses, hats, shoes, stockings, and blouses.

My sisters and I had rummaged through these clothes before while playing in the attic. Every kid plays dress-up at one point in their lives. Adults do it too; it's called Halloween.

This time, I was up there in the cold attic alone, in secret, dressing like a woman. A few adults do that too; it's called something else.

I found a dress that fit me, a jacket, a scarf, pumps, gloves, and even nylon stockings. This was before pantyhose, so I had to keep them up with rubber bands.

During the whole process, thoughts were racing through my head; was I really going to go through with this? Would Mom spot me before I made it out the door, or worse, Dad? How would I ever explain what I was about to do, or why I thought it was a good idea? I didn't want to dwell on that now; I still had work to do on my face.

Downstairs, I rummaged through Mom's eye makeup, powders, and rouge and did my best applying it to my face. I even threw on a necklace, making me look like a rather short Gypsy. Lastly, I rubbed on the lipstick, "kissed" the toilet paper like I'd seen Mom do a hundred times and walked out the door having absolutely no idea how this was going to turn out.

I walked north on Hill Avenue alone and feeling way more comfortable than I should've been. I got a couple of honks and hoots, but kept going. Walking up to the door, I could smell dinner being prepared. I took a deep breath in the cold late afternoon air, rang the doorbell, and waited for the girls to answer. The long strings of beads around my neck were accentuating the thumping of my heart.

The door opened. Peggy and Rhonda stood there in silence for a moment and in total disbelief. They knew who I was in an instant. As far as I was concerned, I had laid everything on the line. This could have gone either way; glory or disaster.

I could not have been more surprised or pleased by their reaction. Laughing and squealing, they dragged me inside. I'd never heard Peggy squeal before in delight, only in disgust which had been related to my nose blowing incident.

The three of us quickly decided I was supposed to be Peggy's long lost aunt, so we went with that. They introduced me to Rhonda's mother, and we all sat down for a conversation. I used a falsetto to add to the charade and actually believed I was fooling her mother. The girls kept shrieking and laughing so much I was taken aback by what a tremendous success this had become. Who would imagine such a stunt could possibly turn out to be anything but an embarrassing train wreck; a well-deserved one?

This was a side of Peggy I hadn't witnessed before, and I was glowing with it. I had pleased her and, in turn, this was pleasing me.

They made me stay until Rhonda's father, an attorney, came home so I had to keep the farce going long enough to fool him. I knew this man, and I'm sure he knew me right away, but he went along with the game until it was time for me to go. They politely asked me to stay for dinner, but I was exhausted by this time and declined. Besides, the rubber bands holding up my nylons had cut off the circulation to my legs, effectively numbing my feet. Without much feeling below my knees, I hobbled out the door, now resembling a short tipsy Gypsy.

An additional element in all this was I didn't remember stuttering one time during this entire episode. Pretending to be someone else and speaking in falsetto didn't trigger the blocks I normally had. This probably coincides with stutterers being able to sing without a problem, assuming they have the talent in the first place. A singer all my life, I can attest to this.

I always carried a tune, as they say. I'd be belting out, "Oh What a Beautiful Mornin'" from *Oklahoma!* while riding my bike. I sang in the hallways at school, in the bathtub, whenever I was hunting, walking around town, or exploring around the lakes. It annoyed any hunting partners to be sure. I joined any organized singing group that would have me. I could be a fluent person when I was singing. It was my one source of refuge; an escape from my prison, a place I could be where sounds coming out of my mouth were maybe admired instead of ridiculed. I needed this one gift and was thankful for it.

When I got home from Rhonda's, I presented myself to my family, who were already sitting at the dinner table. Everyone laughed but Dad, who just shook his head. He'd been conditioned to expect almost anything when I came home, but not this. I suspect Rhonda's father gently told her that it might be wise to never let that strange boy into his home again.

From the horror of living a nightmare in a light blue dress, to a dream fulfilled in nylons and pumps three years later, I just proved that life can be funny when you're a kid.

By the way, that's the last time I ever wore a dress.

# CHAPTER FOUR

# THE CANDY APPLE MAN

Every year, not long after school started, a much-anticipated event would occur, ranked right up there with Christmas. In truth, it was impossible to knock Christmas off the top spot, but a legitimate contender would be the Spencer Fair. Officially called the Clay County Fair, but because it was located in the Town of Spencer, about twenty miles south of Okoboji, we called it the Spencer Fair.

The fair was nothing short of a great big gift for just being a kid and being alive; a pure gift because I certainly didn't do anything to deserve it. The school board would even cancel classes for a day, usually a Monday, so we could help kick-off the start of Fair Week. Of course, attending on Saturday was a given. Nothing was more important than going to the Spencer Fair.

Mom would drive all four of us kids down to Spencer around noon on Monday and give Mike, my brother, and me each a five dollar bill to spend any way we wanted. This came with no restrictions whatsoever except one; this was all the money we would get from her, and it had to last through Saturday's trip, too. If we spent it all on cotton candy and caramel apples in fifteen minutes, most of our fun was over. She kept my sisters, Marcia and Debbie, with her and let Mike and me fend for ourselves, sometimes never to see them again until it was time to go home some ten hours later.

It's difficult imagining a more joyous time than walking around the fairgrounds with five bucks to spend however we saw fit. Sometimes life is like that. Our bliss should have been tempered with a little twinge of undeservedness, spilling over into humble thankfulness, but we had things to do and see. We would be humble and thankful on the way home. All while trying to talk her out of more money for Saturday's trip back to the fair.

What to do first? This was an easy call because it became routine. Mike and I would make a beeline for the foot-long hotdog stand. Nobody knows why a foot-long hot dog is better tasting than a regular one, but it is. The hot dog place also specialized in fresh squeezed lemonade, each costing thirty-five cents. The foot-long was a no-brainer, but we could get two of them to eat and find a hose bib somewhere and wash them down with water. This was a decision we had to make for ourselves, and most times we'd choose the lemonade; not because we were hot and thirsty yet, but because it was our decision to make. Truth be told, I usually did what Mike decided to do.

We each had $4.30 left and a whole day to blow it. Neither of us was too concerned about Saturday's trip back to the fair. We'd worry about that when the time came.

Next, we looked for the best Midway game ever invented; the *Crane Digger*. It was set up in an elevated tent on trailer wheels. Around the perimeter of the trailer frame, there were twenty individual glass boxes mounted at eye level. Each of those was the size of a large fish aquarium in length and width, but taller at two and a half feet. I've never seen the Crane Digger anywhere other than at this fair. Each glass box was equipped with a small dredging crane. The bottom of the tank was loaded with everything essential to anyone.

These priceless treasures would make excellent possessions; a set of jacks, a miniature deck of cards, pencil erasures, pens, sticks of chalk, shoestrings, and rubber knives.

The cranes were operated by two small metal wheels, one to swing it around and one to lower and raise the bucket claw. We paid the man a dime, and he would turn it on.

The best part of this game, besides the array of precious goods waiting to be mined, was there wasn't a time limit. The crane was all mechanical, so it was a bonafide test of skill. We could spend all day on one dime if we wanted. The excitement created by the possibility of grabbing the ten dollar bill attached by a rubber band to a heavy stone was always there. The fact that it was tucked back in a corner just out of reach of the crane's claw would usually ensure several attempts made and dimes spent, before my realization of the futility of any successful outcome of that prize. As always, the lure of the cash prize whittled down my remaining nest egg.

After several attempts at the ten-spot, I would lower my sights on the other fine and more accessible gems. Such as a copper boot, a finger trap made in Japan, an assortment of rings with the ever-pinching adjustable band, a three-legged glass unicorn, or a pair of pink sponge dice.

Mike scooped up an excellent keychain with the three see no evil monkeys in a row. This would come in handy for him since he found a key once while walking home from school. There were watches, too, but they must have been glued to the bottom.

As far as I was concerned, this was the only place to be at the fair. After about an hour and a half, however, the lure of the *Roc-O-Plane* beckoned us to leave our beloved cranes. I took my precious winnings; a solid gold tie clip, a genuine silver thimble, and an empty Goofy Pez dispenser, and let the cranes rest for a while. We knew we'd be back to inflict more financial damage on the crane man later. We each had just over two dollars left, and it was only two-thirty in the afternoon.

The Roc-O-Plane was my favorite ride. It was sort of a Ferris wheel with egg-shaped cages that were all beat up, as most of the old rides were. Half the lights were out, giving it a rather creepy outline at night. The operator would slam the steel bar down onto our laps in what was already a tight squeeze, even for a person of my age. I often wondered if prison was a lot like this when first walking into a cell. This was about the time I had second thoughts about jumping into this thing.

Mike controlled the lever that acted as a brake releasing the cage so it could spin around independently of the main frame. Keeping the brake intact would cause us to turn upside-down along with the massive wheel. Timing the release of the brake would allow the cage to spin on its own at greater speed.

Mike liked doing whatever made me make the most distorted face while pleading, unsuccessfully, with the toothless grinning operator to please stop the ride each time we passed him at the bottom. Maybe the man just didn't hear me.

When we exited the cage, the horror was over, and I began the job of gathering up any self-respect I could muster. Curiously enough, Mike never walked away wearing my foot-long hot dog all over his shirt. Too bad.

We made our way up the Midway with all the barkers calling me "young man" and pretending they knew me. The ground was a packed-dirt surface, which still provided adequate dust in the drier days later on in the week. Walking by all the food stands was more torture than it was pleasant. The sweet aroma of caramel popcorn hung in the air; along with corn dogs, cotton candy, turkey legs, hamburgers and a relatively new food in the mid-west, pizza. No one seemed to be interested in eating pizza in Iowa, the lines were always short. Our excuse for not trying it was purely a lack of funding. Smelling was all we could afford.

We worked the game booths next. Some of these were the Ring-the-Bottle, Milk Bottle Throw, Balloon Darts, and the Three Softballs into the Basket scam. This softball game was one I seemed to have great skill and success playing, but interestingly enough, only when they allowed me to practice for free. When it was paid for and on the line, I guess I'd get a little nervous because I could never get the third ball into the basket. I couldn't figure that out. Mike suggested they were big cheaters, and it was rigged, but I wasn't convinced. They were so friendly to me, and most grown-up men I didn't know were never nice to me or any other kid.

We were getting down to our last dollar, and we needed a snack. At the Spencer Fair, that meant only one thing; *Tom Thumb Donuts*.

The donut stand was self-contained in some sort of trailer, and it had the complete donut making machine in full view for all to see. The tiny morsels came oozing out of the hopper in rows of ten and fall into the deep fat fryer where they'd then float down like little inner tubes while turning brown. A flipper would turn them over to brown on the other side, then onto the chain conveyor belt to be either sprinkled with cinnamon or powdered sugar.

There was always a waiting line, so we'd be standing behind mostly heavy set people while being engulfed in the sweet aroma of deep frying donuts. By the time we made it to the front of the line, it was as if we hadn't eaten for two weeks. I was always worried they would run out before we got ours.

A dozen of these heavenly morsels would almost deplete the rest of our funds, and a dozen was never enough. We needed a drink by this time, and an ice-cold Coke did the trick. With our money all but gone, we had nothing to do but walk around and watch all the lucky stiffs have fun.

Sometimes we bumped into Mom and the girls and would make plans to meet before we went home. Watching other people have all the fun just because we blew our bundle usually led us to seek out the livestock tents. Mainly because it was free and maybe we might get lucky and see a cow take a big crap on the floor.

Sometimes there was a champion bull with huge bull assets or a monster sow spread out on the straw-strewn floor while twelve piglets scrambled to get their share of mom's milk. There was always a smaller piglet that seemed to get knocked around and pushed out of the free lunch. I'd always feel sorry for it and want to get involved in solving the injustice of it all. I'd berate the piglets for being such, well...pigs. This was not totally unlike standing in line at the donut stand.

On occasion, we would see some kid with a 4-H hat hosing off a cow's butt, which was always sort of cool. It's the only time I ever saw a clean one.

Dad told me once that the livestock show was the actual reason for having county fairs, but I knew he had to be pulling my leg. There was just no way people would ever come to a fair to see a bunch of cows … clean butts or not.

One excellent thing about the Spencer Fair was that the organizers brought in some of the strangest sideshows. One year an exhibit claimed to have a living man from Borneo. I pronounced it "Barnio," but close enough. He was a real guy. Maybe he was actually from Detroit, but it didn't matter. He was a small man with long white stringy hair on his head and thick hair covering his body. He moved around in the straw in his livestock-like pen which was behind the front screen where the barker called everyone in to see this sad little fellow for twenty-five cents.

We stood on a wooden walkway that was slightly elevated, so we were looking down into the pen. The Borneo man shuffled like a chimpanzee; quick short bursts, stopping only to inspect something he'd find on the floor, usually a cigarette butt, which he would eat. He seemed to do this all day; at least he did every time I saw him. He reminded me of a Morlock from the old *Time Machine* movie with Rod Taylor and every boy's new love, Weena, portrayed by Yvette Mimieux. Whenever the pathetic little creature and I made eye contact, I turned away, embarrassed that I was gawking at him in his misery. Try doing that exhibit today.

Once, the fair had a two-headed, mature cow on display. I was disappointed after paying my money and finding it was already dead and stuffed. Out on the tattered canvas sign, above the large graphic "ALIVE!" was a faded and much smaller graphic, "once."

Of course, what would a great fair be like without the dancing girls? Apparently there was no law against young boys gathering around with all the big guys and wondering what the heck was going on. I was uncomfortable standing there. The overall mood of a fun fair was nowhere to be found in this particular area. Nonetheless, everyone else in the crowd seemed to be enjoying themselves or pretending to be.

The black fishnet stockings the ladies wore had holes in them, some darned, but most not. They never smiled. The barker was missing several teeth, so maybe they were, too. Their wigs were lopsided and their shoes scuffed. By nightfall, it got chilly, so I was truly sorry for them.

Apparently, the dazzling show was inside the tent. I was under the impression that the show the girls performed inside the tent was whatever they had just done on the outdoor stage, which wasn't much more than just standing around and shivering. I wasn't sure why anyone would pay to see the same performance the second time when they could just wait for an hour and see it again out here for free. Maybe it was warmer inside the tent.

Nonetheless, I was embarrassed to be there. I felt dirty. It was time to find something else to do.

The Saturday night stock car races were the crowning event of the fair. The roar of the old engines could be heard all over the fairgrounds. There was an old wooden stadium seating area on one side of the racetrack, and for a town like Spencer, it was pretty good sized. The hot rods were always old black cars from the thirties and forties without mufflers.

The deafening noise promised an exciting event, and many accidents happened so the crowd was always pleased. Every time someone wrecked their car there was a collective hush in the stadium, which would break out into wild applause. It was thrilling to watch.

It smelled like burning rubber and dirt, from which the track was made. The races would drag on for an hour and a half while the voice on the loudspeaker yelled what everyone could plainly see for themselves. The announcer behind the microphone would get the crowd on their feet by screaming, "Ladies and gentlemen, here comes Bobby Snare clear from behind, trying his darnedest to knock Jeb Hathaway out of the lead.

"Oh my, what a move! Old Jeb's not making it easy for him, that's plain to see.

"Oh, my! He nearly bought the farm that time. They're coming around the last turn to the checkered flag, and it's gonna be close. Look out! Look out! Oh, my! Jeb just rammed his Dodge right into the side of Bobbie's '43 Ford. That's gotta frost ya!

"Here they come, here they come, blazing to the finish line. It's gonna be close. And it's Jeb Hathaway the winner, ladies and gents. What a race, what a race!

"Wait a minute. Wait a minute, ladies and gentlemen. Bobbie's not done with Jeb yet. He's still chasing him, and he's trying to run him off the track. Ladies and gentlemen, I'm sorry you have to witness this unsportsmanlike conduct.

"Oh my, Jeb's Chevy just took a jolt from Bobby. It looks like both cars are just sitting there on the track. What's this? Both men are climbing out of their windows. We may have a fight on our hands here, ladies and gentlemen. Both crews are running out to the boys and will try to separate them before it gets ugly.

"Okay, I think this might be over. Yes, yes, they're shaking hands now. I guess it's over; they're both walking back to the pit area. Both of their women are running up to join the drivers.

"Oh my, Jeb's wife just decked Bobbie's girlfriend! They're pulling them apart now. Man, what a night at the fair!"

After a while, there would be a massive cloud of dirt and rubber in the air over the crowd, and it would gently sift down into our hair, and onto our skin, and clothes. Everyone felt dirty.

I felt dirty for the second time that night.

With the races over, it was time to go home. Since I was tired, filthy, and broke, I was more than ready. On the Saturday session of the fair, Mike and I would meet Dad, Mom and the girls at some predetermined location and maybe have one last treat on the folks.

---

Like me, Dad had a real love affair with this place. He had attended since he was a kid. I always found that hard to believe, since I figured the fair was a newer novel idea since I came on the scene. Dad always wanted to make a go of it with some money-making scheme. For a few years, he had a nine-hole miniature golf course set up there. Another time he sold fish sticks on a stick and fish patties on a bun, but I never knew how these ventures panned out for him. Sorry to say, I never talked to my dad about stuff like that or much of anything else, for that matter.

There was one idea he could not convince Mom into allowing him to do. Although Dad was the breadwinner of our family, Mom was the bill payer and had a better idea where we were with our finances.

I remember one night they were having a rather heated discussion on Dad's latest proposed venture. The fair was coming up soon, and he wanted to open a stand and sell frozen chocolate covered bananas on a stick. It would only cost $500 to swing the deal and we would all be rich. I never knew Mom to stand her ground when Dad had something he wanted to do or buy, but for some reason on this one, she did. He even went so far as to embellish the pitch with why this unbelievable opportunity was even available.

He actually said to her, "Lee, the guy made so much money in this business, he went crazy, so he has to sell it!"

Well, I bought it, but Mom just laughed at him. Knowing he had stepped over the line of believability, he couldn't even keep a straight face on that one.

She agreed to a taste test using us kids as Guinea pigs. Dad and Mike made a night trip to the store to pick up chocolate chips, bananas, and some caramel apple sticks. We melted the chips in a saucepan and dipped in the halved bananas so that each was fully covered. These went into the freezer for the night. The next day we each had one, or rather, we each had a bite of one and threw the rest away. No chocolate banana stand for Dad.

———————

One particular year, as we were leaving the fair after the races, we stopped by a candy apple place for one last treat. It happened that Dad knew the guy behind the counter from the old days. Dad asked him how he was doing, and the man struggled to complete a simple sentence. The poor fellow tried for some time, but he just couldn't do it. Dad's friend was a stutterer, he stammered; he was, as I knew the term all too well, a stutter box.

I watched him in complete and utter horror while he got our apples. Everyone else seemed to be totally oblivious to what had just transpired. What I had witnessed and now realized was that this degrading curse of speech disfluency would not magically go away when I grew up.

I had never heard an adult, a real live grown-up, stutter before. I had foolishly convinced myself that everything would be alright, and my problem would cure itself, given enough time. I thought there would be major magical mileposts I would pass that would get me into the no-stutter zone.

I assumed some big event like starting junior high or at least high school would end it. After all, no one stutters in high school, or maybe turning sixteen would be the golden ticket because I'd be driving a car then and dating. I certainly wouldn't be dating and stuttering, both at the same time.

If not by then, surely after graduation and entering college; after all, can anyone imagine a stuttering college student? There can't be such person. The big kahuna was; who would marry a man who couldn't say his own name most of the time?

As we left, I overheard Dad say to Mom, "Well, he still has that same damn problem."

Everyone was eating their apples and walking out the gate while talking about how much fun they had had. I walked behind them, my eyes and mouth were wide open, my ears were hot and buzzing, my candied apple was hanging down around my leg. My adolescent dream world had just come crashing down in spectacular flames. It was never going to miraculously end. I was a stutterer, and I was screwed.

I walked away wondering; when I grow up, will I have to be a candy apple man, too?

# CHAPTER FIVE

# COUSINS AND A DEAD PIG

What can be said about cousins? They're in a class all their own as far as kid relationships go. Cousins are not friends or siblings. Friends come and go, and siblings just belong. No matter what disagreements I may have had or what dirty tricks I would play on my brother or sisters, they seemed to forgive and forget; at least while we were still kids.

Cousins are different, probably a little less forgiving if the truth be told, but no matter what our opinions were of each other, there was always the excitement associated with the anticipation of seeing them. Giddiness would be more like it.

My father was one of six children born to Hartman and Anna Andersen. Hartman came over from Denmark with two of his brothers in 1906. He soon went back and married Anna, who apparently had worked for the family in their bakery and brought her to America in 1913 to start their new life in their new country.

They settled in Clay County, Iowa. Hartman began working in the milk and cheese business but finally ended up owning the only general store in the small Iowa town of Gillette Grove with a population of maybe two hundred souls. It was the only store around, doubling as a post office.

Hartman and Anna had three girls and three boys, my dad being number five with a sister after him. All but one remained in the Clay County area. These six siblings brought nineteen cousins into my world to play with. We saw one another when our parents got together or when my folks sent me packing to spend a week with relatives.

The cousins were all close in age, with my brother Mike being the oldest. In those days, all the returning soldiers came home after the war and started families. Our parents were no different.

Even though we lived relatively close to each other, it was always exciting when we got to see the rest of the family. This would pretty much occur on the major holidays; Thanksgiving, Christmas, Fourth of July, and Easter.

Once the parents decided which home to invade, we were off to the races. As long as Hartman or Anna were alive, Christmas was always at their home in Gillette Grove, but other than that everyone else took turns hosting. Probably the most fun was when our gatherings were at Uncle Jack's farm. Jack Holiday had married Dad's younger sister, Jeanette.

At the farm, there was just so much crap to get into (and damage) without incurring too many consequences. We could chase pigs and chickens and watch the cows do what they do best. There was always the hay barn where we played tag, then itched for hours afterward, but it was worth it. We seemed to spend more time out there than at any of the other homes. Maybe it was because Jack had milk cows and he needed to slip away and milk them in the evening. A farmer with dairy cows is pretty much married to them, or in prison because of them, depending on one's point of view. They had to be milked twice a day, like it or not.

There was one particular time when we were guests on the farm and, as luck would have it, it was the Fourth of July.

---

A little background: Mike and I always looked forward to the Fourth of July no matter where we were. This was a day of empowerment for a boy. We'd save up our lawn mowing money knowing that the firecracker man would be coming to town. There were no commercial fireworks stands by the side of the road then. This man would hole up in someone's spare room like drug dealers do today.

We'd hear about him through some friend of a friend of a friend and make our way over there. The suspense of finding this guy and gazing at his wares added to the mystique of the holiday. We didn't need a secret password to get in, just money. What fun is there in buying fireworks right out in the open with a credit card? Here was a slightly shady character in a small rented room with nothing but a bed and a toilet down the hall.

On the bed, and the floor, and against the walls, spread out in full glory, was every conceivable firework we could ever want. We always went for the familiar ones, though. This guy had cherry bombs packed in sawdust for ten cents apiece. These were by far the most powerful explosives we could get, the Mecca of Mayhem.

Eyeball in size, red in color with a green fuse, and they were waterproof. Many a vandal has been expelled from his school for flushing a lit cherry bomb down a toilet. They were called cherry bombs for a darn good reason. They really were bombs. Those babies could take off your hand.

He had M-80's, too. These were about the size and shape of a small Tootsie Roll, maybe a little thicker, glossy gray in color with a fuse centered on the side. Sometimes we referred to them as ash cans; it depended on who we were talking to. M-80's, though not as beloved as cherry bombs, could also take off your hand.

Roman candles, pop bottle rockets, the big display rockets and an array of plain old firecrackers, snakes, smoke bombs and pinwheels adorned his room everywhere we looked. It was an honor just being there.

We went for the big dangerous ones first, the cherry bombs and M-80's. With what money we had left to splurge, we bought the less powerful firecrackers; Zebras, Black Cats, and Lady Fingers. Pop bottle rockets were always excellent for battles or scaring pigs and chickens. We never went much for the big display stuff. It was too expensive compared to all the rest, but mainly, we couldn't blow stuff up with them. We were after destruction, pure and simple.

---

Let's go back to the farm: Here we were, all of us cousins, loaded for bear and about to take on Jack's farm on the Fourth of July. Jupiter had aligned with Mars.

All the families arrived about noon. It was Iowa hot, but no one cared. After the obligatory greetings; the yelling, the back-slapping, and the unveiling of our mastery of any new flatulence sounds since we last met, we eventually pulled out our stash of explosives and compared the quality.

Our firecracker standards were pretty high. It was always dicey to introduce a new one into the mix and risk being verbally abused as a poor connoisseur of the product line. When disagreements occurred, we'd have a blow-up contest. Usually, a tin can first or a bucket. If the new brand wasn't up to snuff, the red-faced novice was soundly ridiculed. We then marched on our quest of blowing stuff up.

The horizontal part of a clothesline post was usually made from a three-inch iron pipe, so it was always inviting to stuff a few firecrackers in there since it shot out of both ends. Even if a sparrow had had the misfortune of building a nest there, it didn't matter. It was July, the nests were probably empty. At least they were when we were done.

A bunch of giggling boys at a wide open farm with ammunition and a glowing punk (used to light fuses) generated a sense of reckless power in all of us. We blew up everything that would look different if it were blown up.

Lighting one under a rock was a waste of a good round. The younger kids usually had ideas like that. Their keen sense of mischief had yet to develop.

They'd blurt out, "Hey, let's put one under the barn door!" or "Hey, let's put one on top of that log!"

We hated to stifle their enthusiasm, but give me a break. "Put one on top of a simple log?" The older kids knew all these novices needed was to be taught well by the Masters; us.

We put cherry bombs under buckets and watched them blow twenty feet into the air. We'd make the old tried-an-true nestling-cans mortar launch system, where the smaller can-missile reached sixty feet in the air.

It was always fair game to throw firecrackers onto the ground behind a little kid. He wouldn't lift up twenty feet like a can or anything, but he probably thought he had. After a couple of hours, we even started wedging them into cracks in the barn or under the tractor or other equipment, not expecting too much to happen. I hated to admit it, but repetition and a certain lack of imagination did cause a slight digression in our destruction activity.

A cherry bomb placed in the middle of a big old cow pie was always good for a laugh. We also used the smaller loads to blow these things up. Sometimes the fuses didn't always work, and we were left with a dud. It's always a risky play to relight a fuse on a dud because there wasn't much of a fuse left to light. At the same time, we didn't want to waste a perfectly good firecracker either.

Once we had a Zebra brand firecracker in a fresh green cow pie and waited for it to explode. It didn't, and I volunteered to tend to it. The fuse had touched some of the juiciness of the pie, and it had gone out. I kneeled over it and touched my glowing punk to the remainder of the fuse. Do I even need to finish this story? I've never heard such wicked laughter as was generated from what were supposedly good kids.

As I said before, repetition brings on monotony, and even the power of explosives can get boring. We were running out of stuff to blow up.

We were walking back in the direction of the farmhouse when we saw it.

In a grove of poplar trees, lying on the ground was our "golden calf." Actually, it was a big dead pig. A big dead pig with all sorts of orifices. Jack must have discovered it early on in the day lying in the pen and dragged it out there. It was still fresh enough to approach.

Sometimes the heavens spill forth blessings without explanation, and all you can do is offer thanks. Then take full advantage of the gift. Not only did we find a dead fresh pig, but we found it with all the cousins present and on the Fourth of July when we were loaded with explosives.

Oh, the possibilities! We jammed his nostrils first with Black Cats and Zebras. The explosions ripped his nose off. We then jammed more into each of his ears. There was nothing much left of them after that. We saved the M-80's and cherry bombs for his mouth. We stepped way back, awaiting the result. The roar was deafening. Teeth and jaw bones were raining down on us like cats and, well... pigs.

All the while we were laughing uncontrollably and trying hard to catch our breath. Our sides ached, and there was nothing we could do about it. We were holding on to each other to prevent us from falling. This activity drove us all into some sort of laughing frenzy, all the while knowing the best was yet to come.

With the pig's head destroyed to our satisfaction and pretty much beyond recognition, we focused on the other end. We stuffed several of the less powerful firecrackers into his last remaining orifice. Not too much resulted in this, but it was one of the funniest things any of us had ever seen. Our sides still aching and almost unable to speak, we found a stick and rammed in a cherry bomb. We tried to get one of the little cousins to do it with his hand, but no dice. We lit the fuse and ran for cover.

That was the moment all of us knew for sure why you never hold a cherry bomb too long before you throw it. To be crude, we had blown that pig a new one. We were all grabbing our own butts and wondering what that must have felt like.

With the excitement of seeing our cousins when we arrived at noon, we had forgotten about lunch, and now we were all starving.

Back to the house we went, laughing and holding our sides. Our Fourth of July had come to an end except for the pinwheels, Roman candles, and sparklers at dark. After all, what would the Fourth of July be without sparklers at the end?

More important, how would we ever top this year?

We never did.

# CHAPTER SIX

# TWO ROLLS AND A PEPSI

Thousands of boys across the nation have had paper routes. For many it was their first experience in the business world, and I was no different. My brother Mike was first to have one since he was almost three years older than I.

He started out with a morning route, the *Des Moines Register*. He'd set his alarm for five-thirty in the morning to get to the movie theater by six, where the papers were dumped off every day. I admired him for his determination and dedication, especially when he added a second route, an after-school one, with the *Spencer Reporter*.

His alarm clock was, well, most alarming and didn't have the capability of slowly waking him with soft music. The clock had a miserable deafening buzzer, not unlike those used today at basketball games. For years, this alarm was a daily reminder that I never wanted to be a paperboy.

That all changed when Mike wanted to go to Boy Scout Camp (or mosquito-frenzy week) and asked if I could take over his route while he was gone. I was pleased he asked since he was showing some well-hidden confidence in me, but at the same time, I was leery of the responsibility and the alarm clock.

In the end, I agreed to do it. To learn the route, I followed him around on his deliveries the week before he left. Of course, there was no pay associated with this training period, but he introduced me to a slice of heaven that more than made up for it.

To my delight, midway through the route we made his routine morning visit to a little café called Smokey's. The name didn't have anything to do with the air quality in this greasy spoon though it certainly could have. Smokey was the owner's nickname.

We sat at one of the old worn red plastic-covered booths on the left side of the room. Smokey came from behind the long dining counter dressed in a white t-shirt, sleeves rolled up with a pack of Camel straights tucked into the left one. He wore a soiled dish towel around his waist in place of an apron. He was medium height, not overweight, with thinning black greasy hair. I guess he didn't believe the Bryllcream lady on TV that claimed, "A little dab will do ya."

Marty Robbins' "El Paso" was playing on the jukebox. I felt proud and halfway grown up just sitting there.

He laid the silverware onto the table, and Mike spoke, "Smokey, meet my little brother, Doug. He's taking over the route while I'm gone."

He shook my hand and asked with a smile, "What will you have, as if I have to ask?"

"Two rolls and a Pepsi for me, and the same for my brother," Mike answered.

I'd been hearing about this "two rolls and a Pepsi" thing for some time now, and I was definitely looking forward to finally trying it out for myself.

"You got it, Mike," he said as he made his way back behind the counter.

I had heard Mike mention this guy before in a positive way, and now that I'd met him, I could understand why. He didn't treat us like stupid kids, but as bonafide customers.

We were to get our own bottles of pop from the floor cooler in the corner which was filled with cold water. The bottles were submerged in the water while hanging on rows of metal racks. We guided them along the racks and out the dispenser end. We opened the twelve-ounce bottles on the opener attached to the side of the cooler and went over to the jukebox to check out some of the selections.

We weren't going to actually pay for any songs, but it was always fun to recognize some we knew. We were counting on some of the other customers, mostly farmers, to pony up. Three songs for a quarter was just too steep for a paperboy, especially when we could order two rolls and a Pepsi for thirty cents. Three dimes was all Smokey was ever paid since the concept of tipping was lost on any kid our age.

Smokey was bringing the rolls over to us, so we headed over that way and settled into our booth.

"Hope you enjoy them, too, Doug," he said.

There they were; two of the biggest cinnamon rolls I'd ever seen, topped with icing and a big glob of butter melting into a crater of yellow liquid. The rolls were warm; he made them fresh every day, and these had just come out of the oven, hot and steamy. We gobbled them down like ravenous dogs, saving the cold Pepsi for last. There was nothing better, absolutely nothing better.

The Big Bopper's, "Running Bear" sung by Johnny Preston was playing now, and our stomachs hurt. We both provided a big belch. It was time to continue on our route. We paid Smokey our thirty cents apiece and walked out the door. Now that I had experienced the famous two rolls and a Pepsi, I would seriously have to reconsider my objection to having my own paper route.

Later on, I did take over Mike's morning route, and I had thirty to forty papers to deliver before school. On Friday afternoons, I would have to cover the same tracks again to collect for the week, riding my bike whenever I could. This kind of work minimized my reliance on having to speak to the public to be successful. However, collection day was still a stumbling block.

Once Dad wanted to know how I asked for the collection money from my customers. I explained to him how I held up the collection book, sort of rattled it in front of their faces, and blurted out, "Collect!"

Being a people person and the professional salesman he had become, Dad said my approach was rude, and I should consider changing it to, "May I collect, please?"

Of course, I knew he was right, but apparently he still didn't understand my particular predicament. Before I knocked on any door, I'd be repeating, "C-c-c-c-collect, C-c-c-collect, C-c-c-collect, collect," under my breath several times to get the stutter out. Once the customer's door opened, my brain wasn't blocking on the hard cl word, "collect," anymore. Stutterers have a gamut of tricks that help them get out of embarrassing situations. I needed to go through this routine with every single stop.

One of the more common dodges I used in everyday situations was the "bait and switch" technique. I might be doing my best in telling a story to someone about a boat rudder. The word "rudder" would have been a stumbling block word for me. As I was telling the story, I knew all the while that the word rudder was naturally going to have to come into the conversation.

I could see it coming down the conveyor belt of discourse. The word rudder would be coming up soon, and while I was talking, I was thinking of some other word to substitute for it that might be easier to say. I was a walking thesaurus. I might replace the word rudder with, "You know that steering thing on the bottom."

The person I was speaking to would, hopefully, inject the word rudder for me, and I would nod and repeat the word verbatim, as though it had just slipped my mind for a second. I could always repeat a word just spoken by someone. The fear, somehow, had been removed from that word. I would need to repeat the word or phrase immediately, though, to gain the fluency.

This worked for me sometimes, but never when having to introduce someone by name. This was an absolute nightmare, and I avoided it at all costs. Names can't be substituted, and I'd be trapped like a rat if the situation ever presented itself, especially with adults.

The gimmicks come and go, but in the end, every word becomes the impossible word to say.

---

Bear with me as I add a side story here: I even employed this practice technique later on when I was dating a sorority girl at Iowa State in Ames. Her name was Leigh Miller.

Whenever a guy came to pick up his date at the Alpha Gamma Delta house, he was required to speak into a phone receiver which was connected to an intercom. His voice was broadcasted throughout the entire sorority house, a residence filled with seventy-five girls, who were just waiting for a good laugh.

If I had blurted out, unrehearsed, "L-L-Leigh M-M-Miller, y-y-you have a g-g-gentleman c-c-caller,", that disaster would be broadcasting everywhere. I had visions of seventy-four girls running out of their rooms to the railings at the top to the stairs, robes on, curlers in their hair, and peering over the sides. They'd all be trying to get a load of the sorry sap dating poor L-L-Leigh, who would've been hiding in her closet by then.

I had to get this down with a minimum of embarrassment for both her and me; mostly me.

I'd wait until one of the four receivers was available and pick it up, but hold down the hook. If it was a busy night of dating, I'd have to wait so none of the other guys could see what I was doing. When the coast was relatively clear, I began my routine.

For reasons I'll explain later, I didn't stutter when I whispered, so by gently nodding to obtain some sort of rhythm. Taking a deep breath, I would whisper, "Leigh Miller, you have a gentleman caller; Leigh Miller, you have a gentleman caller; Leigh Miller, you have a gentleman caller," into the phone with my finger still on the hook. On the last attempt, I'd let the hook pop up and, with my normal voice, repeat my now-perfect sentence.

This was a lot of work and worry. By-and-large it was easier to date someone else who lived off campus. Leigh was either a victim of the intercom or she dumped me for someone from the university debate team. Either way, life was easier for both of us.

---

Returning to my paper route story: My father now wanted me to rehearse what he had just asked me to say, "May I collect, please?" These four lousy words may as well have been the *Gettysburg Address*. All of my family happened to be in the room since it was dinnertime. He wasn't putting me on the spot to embarrass me, he just wasn't altogether aware of the extent of my disability, and he genuinely wanted to improve my business skills.

I couldn't very well go into my normal indirect way of nodding and whispering practice trials, so I came right out with it, "May I collect, please?" I couldn't believe it. It was a miracle. Something worked! I did it!

In my world, Dad was the most difficult person to talk to. I avoided him because of this sad state of affairs, and it had a quarrelsome effect on our relationship throughout all those years. That was most unfortunate. I'm aware that other people always enjoyed him as a fun and entertaining fellow, but this was the side of him I wasn't privileged to know.

After those perfect words came out, Dad's countenance instantly changed from one of annoyance to that of satisfaction and pride. Through a broad smile, he elated, "Oh, Doug, that sounds so much better."

Something as simple as that moment of approval from my dad is still in my memory some 55 years later.

Having a newspaper route in the Midwest was divided into two categories; the winter route and the non-winter route. Winter in Okoboji is always long and somewhat depressing. We might not see the sun for six to eight weeks in a stretch, mostly gray, cold cloud cover. Sometimes, however, it could be quite enchanting, especially for a young boy.

The dreaded alarm would get me going around five-thirty in the morning, enough time to wrap up in my hat, gloves, long underwear, woolen socks, parka, and boots. I'd throw my newspaper sack over my shoulder and run out the door into the cold.

Sometimes it would still be snowing from a storm that had begun in the night, which created some of the more beautiful memories I have of my morning routine. It was dark at this hour in the winter, and except for a lonely street lamp on each corner, it would've been pitch black.

I could judge how much snow was falling by looking up at the street lamp, which was nothing but a single small bulb hanging in the center of a round metal corrugated shade. It was deathly quiet, and my breathing and crunching footsteps were the only sounds I heard. The accumulated snow on the streets could be anywhere from six inches to three feet, waiting for the snowplow to whisk it away.

After walking around in those conditions for an hour or so, even as cold as it was, I would become thirsty. I'd reach down with my gloved hand, swipe a bit of the new fallen snow, and eat it until my cheeks became numb. All the while knowing what awaited me at Smokey's.

At the mid-way point of my route, I'd make the turn at the same corner every day. I'd see the beckoning lights of the café a couple of blocks away; it was the only place open at that time.

Entering Smokey's while it was still dark outside was delightful. I'd stamp my boots and brush off the snow from my parka before opening the door. The smell of bacon, eggs, coffee and cigarette smoke filled the warm air inside. Smokey would always greet me with a smile and a, "Hey, Doug!"

While walking to my booth, I'd blurt out, "Two r-r-r-rolls and a P-P-Pepsi," and start hanging all my snow gear on the hook by the bench. My shirt would be moist from walking through the snow, and it would steam as it dried in the warm café air. Most times I'd then begin singing along with Pat Boones', "Love Letters in the Sand" or Sonny James,' "Young Love."

The paper route business wasn't a real money maker. I made around ten cents a customer per week, so my enterprise was netting me a whopping four to five dollars weekly, delivering seven days a week and the eighth round for Friday night's collections. That's less than a dollar per day, of which I spent thirty cents a day at Smokey's, leaving me two or three dollars per week for other spending. Somehow, though, it was worth every footstep; but only if everyone paid, which sometimes they didn't.

One of my customers, a single lady, lived alone in the downstairs half of an old house about three blocks from mine. She was never home for my Friday night collection times, and after a while, she was in arrears about eight weeks. I left reminder notes several times on the nail on her door which was actually inside the house in a rather large foyer. She still didn't pay. I would find my notes discarded on the floor.

On one Friday night visit, I brought a red crayon and wrote in big letters all over her white door, "PLEASE PAY THE PAPERBOY, IT'S BEEN EIGHT WEEKS, THANK-YOU." The next week on collection day I was looking forward to an envelope with all my past due money in it. I was a silly boy. When I got there, the door had been scrubbed clean and on the same nail was an envelope with a letter that read, "How dare you vandalize my door! Meet me here tomorrow morning at nine and I will see about paying you."

Needless to say, I never went back there again. The funny thing was, I didn't consider myself a vandal and didn't believe I was malicious at all. Kids are like that, or at least I was.

One mid-November night after collecting on my route, which always took a couple of hours longer than just delivering, I returned home in the dark. I dumped my money out of the green canvas bank bag, which had a snug string sewn around the top. I piled all the coins neatly and stacked the few dollar bills I had on the table. I always knew exactly how many dollar bills I had in my bag because almost everyone paid the thirty-five cents with change. This time, I knew I had only two bills.

I was a dollar short. I didn't have to count it again knowing how many bills I should have. Still, I must have looked into that bag twenty times before turning it inside-out.

Somewhere between my last customer and my home was my dollar bill, just waiting to be picked up by anyone who happened along. I took this pretty hard and complained to Mom it just wasn't fair and that I had worked too hard to lose so much. She was making dinner, but found the time to feel sorry for me. I attempted to get her to feel sorry enough to make up for my loss, but to no avail.

I found the family flashlight and went looking for my dollar, retracing my steps as best as I could remember. Realizing the futility of hunting down a bill in the dark, I made plans to retrace my steps first thing in the morning. I was going to find my dollar. This meant I would need to adjust my established route to accommodate the search. I certainly didn't want some no-account kid to find my hard-earned cash.

When I got up the next morning, I discovered I needn't bother adjusting my route to look for my dollar. Lying on the ground was the first snowfall of the season, about eight inches of it.

Winter was here in Okoboji. It just wasn't fair.

Most Iowans dreaded the coming winters. The dirty piles of snow along the streets, the sunless skies, the barren trees, the bitter cold, the dead car batteries, and the shortened days all made certain misery. In the Midwest, it was time to just hunker down. It would be a long, long wait until spring.

As miserable as it was, there were still moments of charm and haunting beauty.

I received a pair of ice skates for Christmas one year and, after most evening dinners, I walked the five blocks to one of the frozen lakes to go skating. Sometimes the snow melted on the ice during the day and would quickly refreeze again and form a glassy smooth, clear surface to glide upon.

I was usually alone; there was no sound except for the blades skimming over the black ice. The cold, crisp, fresh winter air filled my young lungs. Sometimes the moon would light my way. Other times the sky filled with millions of stars would guide me. Either way, it was enchanting, and I'd skate for hours. These were moments I kept for myself.

One year the city's Kiwanis Club built a splendid toboggan slide on the bank of East Okoboji Lake. The men started construction in late fall, and we watched the progress from time to time after school.

Before the slide, kids would have to make up their own brand of fun in the snow, like finding the biggest hill in town and sledding down it all day. Nothing was ever built for us kids, at least not anything as amazing as this was going to be.

It was a wooden structure with two chutes and stairs that reached more than twenty feet high leading to the two loading platforms, one lower than the other. The elevated toboggan chutes were the width of a toboggan and had two-foot safety panels on each side to keep us on the track. The wooden chutes led down to the frozen lake at the bottom of the hill. The chutes had a thin layer of ice on them to allow the sleds to gain maximum speed.

There was great anticipation among the kids in town, and on the opening weekend, it was jammed with people from every surrounding town as well. Because toboggans were twenty dollars for the cheaper ones and more for a padded one, I concluded that only the lucky stiffs could afford them. I would have to hitch a ride with anyone who was kind enough to take me aboard. The two hardware stores in town were having a heyday selling these things.

One night when our family was eating dinner, we were talking about the new slide and all the fun we were having on it. I don't remember bugging Mom or Dad about getting a toboggan for our family, I just assumed we wouldn't be, at least not a new one.

Dad spoke up. "Doug, why don't you go out on the back porch and bring in the newspaper I left out there?"

I got up and opened the door. There it was, a brand new seven-foot toboggan leaning against the wall. Dark and light hardwood slats finished with a high-gloss shine. It was beautiful.

I yelled, "A t-t-t-toboggan, a t-toboggan!"

The siblings shot out of their chairs to see if I was just fooling them. Loud shrieks and shouts were made as we all ran our hands over the smooth varnished wood. I guess we were now official junior members of the *Lucky Stiffs Club*.

To climb to the top of the slide, we carried our long sleds upright on the icy stairs. On the top platform, we'd lay the sleds down at the starting gate. The slide was monitored by the same group of volunteers who built it. Anywhere from six to eight thrill seekers would climb aboard, link their legs around the waist of the person ahead of them, and hold fast to the safety ropes attached to each side of the sled. We held our breath as they pushed us off. It was an exhilarating ride all the way down to the bottom and out onto the lake. This ride opened at noon and closed at nine in the evening. Surprisingly, there was absolutely no charge.

By the end of the season, in early spring, the crowds had thinned and some of the hours of operation were trimmed. The ice on the chute would melt during the day, and a new layer would have to be applied with a hose for the night crowd.

For a good laugh, boys started building large snow ramps on the lake at the bottom and waited for the next unsuspecting sled group. The ramp would send the toboggan and its occupants airborne, dumping everyone on top of each other.

The volunteer men were becoming less enthusiastic, so security was lax and people were getting hurt. Since this wasn't a money-making venture, I'd guess the Kiwanis Club, the city council, and the mayor were glad to see the season end.

By the time summer came around we were rolling tires, basketballs, and marbles down the rickety chute and watching them disappear into the lake. Unpainted wood doesn't stand up to the weather very long in Iowa, and the graying skeletal-like structure was eventually torn down. Toboggans were being sold on the cheap if they were sold at all.

The first signs of spring are glorious to a kid after a long dark, cold winter. Working a morning paper route magnified that experience. It was one of the perks.

One glorious Sunday morning in early April while delivering my papers, the sun was just rising and melting all the icicles and snow. A few sprigs of struggling green grass were peeking up through some old dirty snow piles left by the plows months ago. Anything green was welcomed. The smell of wet asphalt was in the air from all the snowmelt in the streets. It was a great day to be alive. I'd already stuffed my stocking cap in my coat which was now unbuttoned. Summer was just around the corner; we could taste it, smell it. And summers were everything in Okoboji.

I was near the end of my route and looking forward to Mom's french toast breakfast. I never ate at Smokey's on Sundays, as Sundays were always his busiest day, and I doubted he would miss my thirty cents.

I jumped off the porch of my last delivery and landed in the wet crystallized snow. Something caught my eye. Under a shimmering melting sheet of ice, there he was; George Washington, looking back at me. It was my lost dollar. This was going to be a magnificent summer.

Later on, I changed my morning paper route to an afternoon one. It had a bigger customer base which netted me about seven to eight dollars a week. I delivered after school and in the winter, I wouldn't be home until dark. This was six days every week, with Saturdays off. More money and sleeping in later during the week seemed like a good trade, so I took it.

Mom wasn't as enthusiastic about the change. On some colder nights, I might be running late for all kinds of reasons. I'd stop by the house halfway through the route to whine and beg her to drive me the rest of the way. More often than not, she would reluctantly agree to do it.

She had been standing over a hot stove with several pots bubbling away, making dinner for her four kids and Dad. She'd still take the time to put on her coat, start the old '49 green Buick, and drive me around town in the snow. Mothers are a special breed. I hope I remembered to say thanks.

The afternoon paper was preferred by some customers, even though it was smaller. The reporters could gather all the news of the day and have it in print by nightfall, whereas morning papers could only run stories of the previous day or early evening.

One such newsworthy story made it in the afternoon paper first.

It was February 1959, the third day of the month, and I was delivering the *Spencer Reporter* with headlines that read, "Buddy Holly Killed in Plane Crash Near Mason City, Iowa."

*Bad news on the doorstep.*

I was stuffing myself again with hot cinnamon rolls in Smokey's Café one morning when Smokey asked me to do him a big favor. I couldn't say no since he had been so friendly to me, and I was forever addicted to his rolls. He asked me to take a project off his hands.

I never knew how he got stuck with it, but the task involved delivering a thousand brochures around town, one to every house. Not only that, but I needed to record every address delivered. He would pay me a pitiful penny apiece. I was too spineless to decline, so I stuffed them all into my newspaper bag and went home.

After about a week, Mom prompted me to get started on this endeavor. Smokey had called her and wanted to know how I was doing. I had avoided the café all week, afraid to face him.

I finally started out with good intentions by stuffing the brochures into the doors at the first few houses, but when it came to actually writing down the addresses, I was overwhelmed. I wasn't up to speed on the specifics of the address system. I would never get this done. Write every address in town, onto this form, in sequence as I delivered them, and all for a lousy ten bucks? I figured it would take two months.

I went whining to Mom and convinced her to call Smokey and get me off the hook. I heard her explain to him that due to this special friendship he and I had, I had been too shy to say no when he asked me to do this almost two weeks ago.

He told her to have me bring the fliers back to him, and he'd take care of it. I was greatly relieved and took them directly over. I was anxious to get back to my diet of sweet rolls as soon as possible.

To my surprise and total dismay, he wasn't the old smiley, friendly Smokey I had come to know. I had let him down, disappointed him.

In so many words, he told me it might be best if I didn't come back again.

Until then, I hadn't had an adult express so much bitterness toward me. Not even Ron's mom, Pearl, who had a legitimate beef against me for ruining her mattress, it was most discomforting.

So much for my two rolls and a Pepsi addiction. I would always miss the place.

**The toboggan slide on East Okoboji Lake in Spirit Lake
Circa 1961**

# CHAPTER SEVEN

# CHRISTMAS TIME

Christmas was always a time of great anticipation and excitement. Bringing down the boxes of lights and ornaments from the frigid attic was normally the starting point. It was like seeing old friends again after a long time. Of course, since we were kids, and ornaments were made of thin glass, there were less of them year after year. Our ornament collection was so old the coloring was half gone on most of them.

We'd check the electric bulbs first and replace any that were burned out. We even saved the cheap old tinsel until it wouldn't unravel at all. Of course, all of us kids ended up wearing the tinsel on our heads, pretending to be movie stars.

Buying a Christmas tree wasn't a family affair for us. Whenever Dad decided to take the time to pick one up and haul it home was when the Christmas season officially started in our home. Once the tree was upright and as stable as it was going to be in the three-legged wobbly red and green metal bowl, it was time to load it up.

When all the lights and ornaments were hanging, we started throwing on the tinsel, having never been shown how to place it carefully on each branch. Even if we had been shown, we wouldn't have believed anyone would actually do it that way. Who had that kind of time? Dad always put the angel on top, always crooked, but it wasn't his fault; it was an overweight angel in a rather dirty, white satin robe. One of her eyes had been gouged out, and half her hair was gone. She was quite a sight to look at, but she was our angel, and she seemed to still be smiling through all of the unsolicited abuse.

One year, Dad bought one of those vertical shaped glass ornaments supposed to represent the Star of Bethlehem. He carefully unwrapped it from its shiny new box and proudly attached it to the top of the tree. My sister Marcia felt the pain of the soiled beaten up angel who was left in the bottom of the decoration box. We all sang the first verse of "O Little Town of Bethlehem", the only verse anyone knows by heart. Everyone sang but Marcia that is. The star didn't last the season. The dog brought down the tree one day and the star shattered into a thousand pieces. In truth, we weren't positive it was the dog, but we blamed him anyway. Back up went our tired old angel. Her smile seemed more devious than before. We wondered if she had had any influence on the dog or Marcia.

Our family, like most others, I imagine, would gather all the presents under the tree for two weeks before the big day. My siblings and I separated them into groups of ownership. Mine would be here, theirs would be over there.

We gave it our best shot at x-ray vision by pressing down on the paper and catching any telltale lettering or picture that might give it away. There was always the overwhelming desire to tear a little piece of the wrapping away to get a better idea as to its contents. To my knowledge, it was never done; at least I didn't do it. That would be all-out cheating and definitely frowned upon.

One year, in my relentless desire to discover what I was getting for Christmas, I peeked at Mom's shopping list hidden in her purse. She had written down my name and the word aquarium after it. For some reason, I thought I deserved something much better than stupid fish, and I let her know in a tactful way that I didn't want an aquarium. She was disappointed and surprised by this declaration. That year I got a bunch of socks, a couple of shirts, and a buck-fifty hockey stick. It came without a box, so it didn't take much of a sleuth to figure out what was inside the paper wrapping.

Sometimes I'd almost crush the boxes to get a feel of what might be hiding in there. If a box was lightweight and could be squeezed all the way flat, it was always clothes and didn't really count when it came to claiming the crown for the most presents. These were put to the side in the "it's mine, but who cares pile." We usually got several of those.

It was difficult to determine which one was the grand gift, the "Big Kahuna." If the present was heavy, it was usually a good one, barring any brick-in-the-box trick. It could be anything; a pair of binoculars or a miniature arcade game, even a bicycle. Of course, a bicycle would have to be rolled into the pile during the night so it wouldn't be part of our guessing game. Bikes were an excellent gift, but given the time of the year, they were pretty much useless until spring.

One year my brother Mike got the coolest gift. It was a semi-remote controlled army tank. The tank was tethered to an eight-foot wire with a handheld control box. It went anywhere, except up the stairs. He'd bury it in the snow, then watch it burst out of harm's way. We set up our army men and ran them over and proceeded on to victory. We dug a labyrinth of tunnels and caves into the snow and sent in the mechanical beast to tear them all down.

Everyone on our street wanted one. I wanted one.

My kahuna that year was a semi-remote controlled tractor-trailer, or semi, as we called them then. It wouldn't go anywhere. It just sat there on the icy sidewalk, spinning its useless wheels. The unit would jack-knife when I tried backing it up and it was continually falling over because of the profile-to-wheelbase ratio. I couldn't haul a load with it because the loading doors on the trailer were painted on. Mike and his friends got a lot of ridicule mileage out of it. Eventually, I had to join in on the joke and offer it up as a sacrifice to the King of Toys.

We painted a swastika on the side of the trailer and it became an instant enemy. The poor truck was run over so many times it got boring. I did wonder how this piece of fodder would run on a clean, dry sidewalk in the summer, but it didn't make it through the winter.

My siblings and I bought the usual lame gifts parents get from their kids; the doily for Mom and the screwdriver for Dad, an ashtray from school clay class or painted clothes pins, explaining that they were to hold important letters for the mailman. One year I surprised everyone.

Our house had just been remodeled in the fall. Nothing major, but for us it was a big deal. In reality, all they did was remove a wall in the living room that had no business being there in the first place. It divided a large room into two useless smaller ones with a passageway in the center.

Once that mistake was gone, a rather large lady came over and steamed off all the wallpaper, but not until we had our go at it. The night before, Mom brought out the box of crayons and let us scribble whatever we wanted all over the walls. We were a little hesitant at first because it was such a major no-no, but it didn't take long to get the hang of it.

A new woolen carpet was installed from a remnant batch. It was light in color and always tough to keep clean. Dad bought a new Danish modern sofa with purple striped foam-rubber cushions that sort of matched the new purple-etched wallpaper. The sofa was uncomfortable and butt-ugly, but it was new, so we loved it. Mom added a lamp table on each side of the new sofa, and we kept the old gray sofa-chairs, which faced the new Magnavox stereo/hi-fi/color TV set to complete the room.

I had some money from snow shoveling jobs which came my way that season, and I wanted to do something lavish for Mom. I was thinking of buying two lamps to put on those tables next to the new sofa. She had remarked how nice lamps would look someday when they could afford it. After all, Dad had just spent a wad on the remodel, and I imagined they were feeling underfunded.

About two weeks before Christmas I went shopping in the only furniture store in town within walking distance. I described the changes and the décor the best way I knew how to the sales lady.

"S-s-sort of p-p-purple w-wall p-paper and a p-p-purple sofa," I said. It was too bad it had to be purple. "P-words" always gave me trouble. Of course, blue, red, black, brown, yellow, or white wouldn't have worked either. If only more names of colors started with letter "h." Words that began with h were much easier for me to say. Maybe "hell-of-a-purple" would have worked.

She smiled and pointed to two tall purplish lamps with cylinder-shaped shades. They were perfect, but I assumed much too expensive for me. I told her I had thirty dollars to spend.

Mr. Townshend, the owner, came out to meet me, and the saleslady filled him in on my dilemma. He knew who I was and told me the lamps were fifteen dollars apiece, and he would deliver them for free. I was thrilled. I could not believe my good fortune to have found two perfect lamps for exactly the amount of money I had.

I hope he didn't lose too much on the deal.

I'd never spent this much money at one time in my life. First, I told my sisters, then Mike, and I knew I couldn't keep from telling Mom for two weeks. Finally, I made Mom guess what I got her, and after some major hinting, she did.

She was flabbergasted, but probably hoping I didn't pick out something goofy. At least she wouldn't have to wear them like she did those thirty-five cent daisy earrings I bought her for Mother's Day. She even called Dad at work to tell him about the lamps. I was feeling pretty generous and special.

We called the store to ask them to deliver the lamps so we could enjoy them for the holidays. Neither Mom nor I wanted to wait. They came in big sacks the next day, and we set them up. Mom was beside herself. She called all her friends and told them about her beautiful lamps, a gift from her boy. This was a new and different experience for me. Mom hadn't been that excited since school started in September.

Mom kept those lamps in a prominent spot in her homes until she died almost thirty years later. Dad sent one to me as a keepsake when he moved into a smaller house. It arrived in several pieces; too many to repair.

Sometimes it would snow during school break just in time for a white Christmas. This was an opportune time to be out shoveling as much snow off sidewalks as possible. Lawn mowing was profitable and dependable, even predictable. Shoveling snow, however, was faster and could be done far into the evening. Snow was easy to see in the dark, and I didn't have to buy gas.

One customer I shoveled snow for was Mrs. McFarland. She lived in an old clapboard house down the street from me. Her house was on an elevated lot with concrete retaining walls next to the sidewalk about three feet high with stairs leading to the front door.

This area would always get pounded with snow drifts so I would shovel her walk first while I was still fresh. She also wanted me to clear a path out to her small, dilapidated barn and remove enough snow for the swinging door. This was hard work, but the sparkling snow and the cold, clean, fresh air had its own quiet enchantment to help ease the drudgery.

It was always a little creepy, but interesting, to knock on the McFarland door and collect my dollar and a half. Mrs. McFarland and her spinster daughter, Ruth, would always be working in the kitchen where I entered at the back of the house. I never once saw the front entryway.

Many times they would be seated around a large galvanized wash tub filled with steamy hot water. Water boiled on the old wood-burning stove in the corner of the room. They each had either a duck or a goose on their lap and were busily pulling off feathers, which were piling up around their feet on the ancient linoleum floor. The pungent smell of steamy wet goose feathers was always rather revolting. I wanted to get out as quickly as I could, but I still had a morbid curiosity about whatever activity I found them doing.

Mrs. McFarland looked, in my estimation, to be at least ninety years old, but then kids think everyone older than their parents are ninety or close to it. She had deep-set eyes with darkened sockets, sunken cheeks, three or four long teeth, and a wart on her nose. Her hair was long and white-gray, usually worn up.

Even though she looked like the witches I saw in the movies, she was a kind woman and seemed to have a genuine concern for me, probably imagined. It's a pity I wasn't interested in where older folks came from and what their lives had been like to get them where they were. Today it would be most interesting to know more about her story.

Nonetheless, I envisioned her sitting around that over-sized steamy kettle-like tub when I read the opening scene of *Macbeth* in ninth grade, "Bubble, bubble, toil, and trouble."

Our extended family's Christmas Eve party was held at Grandma's house in Gillette Grove, about thirty-five miles to the south of Okoboji. The trip there was always exciting and mightily anticipated. We'd leave around five in the afternoon. My sister Debbie would sit up in the front seat of the Chrysler with Mom and Dad, since she was the smallest, leaving Marcia, Mike, and me to fight it out in the back seat. I was usually the hump boy.

We had already opened one present before we left. It was a tradition we kept so we had something to show our cousins when we arrived at Grandma's.

The mood was electric. Dad would turn on the radio and sing or whistle whatever was playing, and he seemed to know them all. Dad had been a bugle boy in the war, which may have helped him develop the art of whistling, he had mastered it quite well. I always enjoyed his whistling for two reasons; first, he was good at it, and secondly, I knew he had to be in a good mood. Whistling is impossible to do if you're in a bad mood.

There was always the smell of cigarette smoke associated when driving with Dad. Second-hand smoke was a given no matter whose car we rode in, as most of the men came back from the big war hooked to the gills on nicotine. It seemed to add to the ambiance of the driving experience. Kids, then, didn't wonder *if* they would smoke, but what brand they might prefer. They usually went with whatever their parents used. My dad preferred Winstons, because they "Taste good like a cigarette should."

To get to Grandma's we'd have to get out of Spirit Lake first. This was a bit trickier than it should have been. We'd always take the highway that ran past Dad's place of work, Stoller Fisheries, where Dad had moved his way up to sales manager. He'd stop there more times than not and make us wait for half an hour in the car. We all hated that. Every time we drove past the smelly place without stopping, we gave a collective sigh of relief, Mom included. I always wondered why he felt the need to visit his place of employment on the way to a party. Only recently I figured he probably wanted a little nip with anyone still hanging around the joint. I'm sure Mom knew this too, but didn't want to spoil the party atmosphere by complaining. A head-on collision sure would have spoiled the party.

Arriving at Grandma's house in the bitter cold made the entrance into the warm house all the more sublime. Cousins came running up to greet us, immediately showing us their opened gifts from home. We'd throw our coats onto the huge pile with all the others on Grandma's bed and begin the evening of fun. Grandma would find each of us, grab us by the arms, and have some heavy Danish-accented comment about how we looked. Usually to me, in her accent, she would look up and say, "Dawky, how's da wedder up dare?" She was barely five feet tall, and I was growing like a weed.

The house was decorated about as well as an older woman could do by herself. It was a two story with a small kitchen in the back which led to the only bathroom beyond that. This was undoubtedly added on when they finally decided to bring the toilet indoors, probably just before the war. One item of curiosity was the ping-pong ball she placed into the hole left when they removed the deadbolt from the door, which had been the exterior door before the addition of the bathroom. I pushed the ball too hard one year and it caved in. It stayed like that until she died. The bathroom wasn't heated, so in December, we had to prepare ourselves before we sat down. She reminded us every time we visited to keep the door open when unoccupied so the pipes wouldn't freeze.

The dining room was furnished with a long table and twelve chairs. The living room was in the front of the house, which we entered from the main entrance. The master bedroom was right off the living room and off limits, except for throwing coats onto the bed. The second floor and stairway were wooden and creaked with every footstep.

When the Andersens got together, the event would always start pretty much the same way. Uncle Earling, we knew him as Elling for some reason, would bring cases of Pabst Blue Ribbon beer in long-necked bottles. Elling was the oldest brother and owned the only bar/café in Webb, a tiny town about five miles south of Gillette Grove. Carlo, the second son, would bring a compressed spiced meat called Rullepolse and a grandiose assortment of thinly sliced and dense breads.

Dad would usually bring the cooked shrimp and some weird smelly cheeses. Actually, everyone brought their own version of stinky cheese; I guess it was a contest to see who could out-stink all the others. Grandma would have prepared her specialty, Danish yardsticks, which were fruit-filled, eighteen-inch long pastries. She brought this divine skill over from the old country. Her treat didn't last long.

The adults would spend the entire evening at the big table talking and laughing. All the food was spread out before them, and it made for a merry atmosphere. Every so often one of them would come up with a good story, causing a deafening explosion of laughter, startling the kids. This happened more often as the evening wore on and the beer supply ran low.

It was around this time Dad and his sisters would attempt to sing "Apple Blossom Time" in four-part harmony. The kids would present some kind of talent show to the group as well. One year I'd learned a musical arrangement of "Winter Wonderland" at a school performance. I taught my sisters to back me, and it was the hit of the evening, at least in my opinion.

Since it was cold and dark outside, we kids played games on the floor in the other room. We tried playing the Ouija Board, but cheating ended it. Monopoly was too confusing with everything going on, and chess was out of the question. Usually, we played Old Maid, Go Fish or even Spin the Bottle.

Around midnight, the yawns got pretty serious. It was time to leave. After wading through the stack of coats, we waited for our folks to finish their goodbyes before we piled into the frozen car for the hour ride home. I claimed the big back window above the seat. The steady hum of the engine and the warmth of the heater lulled me into a blissful slumber. I wanted it to never end.

The ride home was all too quick. It seemed I was just getting toasty when we pulled into our driveway. Then the part every kid hated arrived; getting out of a warm car and a sound sleep, shivering into a cold house, and an even colder bed. Sometimes Mom was too tired to ask if I needed to go to the bathroom. Big mistake.

One year the whole Andersen family came to our house on New Year's Day. After dinner, all the cousins went out to explore, and we ended up at the nearest frozen lake. We were all slipping and sliding on the ice, making the best of a dreary, gray, cold day.

We spotted an area under the highway bridge that never froze as thick as the rest of the lake. Ever being the resident clown, I went out too close to the thinner ice edge near the bridge at the suggestions of everyone there.

I heard the sickening sound of ice starting to crack first. The others all backed away; it was then that the stark realization set in; there was nothing I could do to prevent what was going to happen next. I sank all the way in over my head and bobbed up again. I was in such a state of shock, I couldn't feel the cold or catch my breath. I managed to yell for help to a bunch of kids who couldn't believe their good fortune of seeing me almost drown. Everyone was laughing so hard, they didn't seem to sense the possible danger I might be in.

I pulled myself out onto the thicker ice and staggered to the shore. It was then that I felt the full assault of the bitterly cold water quickly turning to ice. My day's adventure was over. By the time I got home, my clothes had frozen to my body.

There were at least fourteen of us on that ice, and I was the only one who fell in. This didn't surprise anyone, least not my dad. When was I going to learn why these silly mishaps always happened to me? It wouldn't be anytime soon.

On the day following New Year's Day we'd help Mom take down the tree, or what was left of it, as most of the needles were on the carpet by now. It was my job to burn the tree in the fire barrel out back. We were much less careful returning the decorations to their containers than we had been removing them. I'd carry the boxes upstairs to the cold attic, stashing them in the corner to await another year for their contents to bring excitement into our lives once again.

Once the floor was vacuumed and all the lame gifts; socks, belts, and pot holders were gathered, it was like it had never happened.

Now all we had to do was endure three more long months of winter, the worst, and by far the longest part of the year.

**Christmas at Grandma's House in Gillette Grove**
**(Anna standing in back)**
**Circa 1960**

# CHAPTER EIGHT

# A BOAT; MY KINGDOM FOR A BOAT

Okoboji in the summer is synonymous with boating, sailing, fishing, water-skiing, and swimming. It's referred to as the Iowa Great Lakes, and most Iowans have spent some time enjoying what it has to offer. From the Town of Spirit Lake, no matter which direction one walks, he'll run into a lake. For a boy, summer is everything in Okoboji.

It was a magical time in my life, filled with promise and anticipation. I'd hit the ground running on the last day of school in the last week of May. The leaves were out, and the lawns had been mowed several times. The depressing piles of dirty snow were a distant memory. So much free time spread out before me and so many possibilities of ways to waste it.

One summer I wanted a boat all my own. Dad hadn't bought one yet, and even if he had, fat chance I would ever get to use it. My friend, Denny Lamplighter, and I were exploring along the shore of East Okoboji one day when we happened to find a wrecked, decaying, wooden row boat. Most boats were made of mahogany wood instead of fiberglass in the fifties. Mahogany was durable in water, but refurbishing was a necessity in the offseason if the wood was to last.

When a boat became too damaged or rotten to warrant repair, it might be scuttled in the middle of the lake or tucked away in some reeds on shore. After all, there was no such thing as a boat junkyard. If it floated, no matter how ugly, it was still a boat and, therefore, had value. However, if it couldn't stay afloat, it was more than likely sunk.

East Okoboji Lake had miles of undeveloped shoreline. Exploring this lake was always a big part of every summer. Any number of items could be found by those willing to walk it. Old anchors, chains, fishing poles or fishing tackle might be scattered around for some alert kid to pack home. Dead fish were also abundant.

My brother, his friends, and I would buy Trident spearheads at the hardware store and attach them to broom handles to spear carp, a plentiful trash fish in this lake. Carp are mud-sucking fish, and East Okoboji has a muddy bottom. This mud was most apparent whenever the lake was lower than usual. After a fall while water skiing, we might be standing up to our ankles in the cold slimy goo lying at the bottom. This was always creepy since I'd heard of mud monsters all my life just waiting for some unsuspecting kid to happen along. It's tough to shake those stories, even as a late teen. My feet dangling in seaweed in the clear blue waters of West Okoboji produced the same uneasiness.

In August, the waters of East Okoboji would be so green with algae it was impossible to actually see the fish. We'd wade into the shallow areas and wait for carp to swim through our legs, and then jam our spear down to where we thought they might be. To my recollection, no one ever stabbed their own foot or someone else's. When we speared one, we'd throw it onto the shore to die and stink for three weeks. Carp were labeled a trash fish and are treated as such. It was always a good time.

Once, I came upon a dead carp that had been out of the water I few days. It was covered with maggots, thousands of them wriggling around and eating his stinking carcass. I found a large flat rock nearby and dropped it onto the fish to see what damage I could do to the disgusting creatures. The slab-like boulder landed in such a way that the entire contents of the fish, innards, maggots, and all, instantly squished up all over my body and face. Horrified, I dove into the muddy green water and ripped off my clothes. Thankfully, I was alone when it happened, or I would've never heard the end of it.

---

So anyway, back to the boat: It wasn't out of the ordinary to find an old discarded boat along the shore. Denny and I surveyed the damage to our boat, which was what we were calling it now. It was extensive. There was a gaping hole in the bottom, but we thought with a little of my Dad's glue and some of his nails, we could easily get it back into the water. We would need some wood, too, which we could get from the scrap pile at the lumber yard. After the repairs were finished, we would need a motor. It was time to find one. After all, we believed in first things first.

We walked to a local bait shop which also sold and serviced outboard engines. It was located on the road that led to Big Spirit Lake north of town. We looked around at all the boat engines in the service area wondering which of these would best suit our needs. Money was no object since we didn't have any.

"W-w-w-we're l-l-looking for a boat e-e-engine," I struggled to tell Big John, the owner.

"Ya, we're looking thor a boat engine," Denny added.

My friend, Denny Lamplighter, had a speech impediment, too. He couldn't make an "F" sound. The word, "friend" would come out "thriend." I used to work on that with him (a classic case of the blind leading the blind). I didn't understand why his tongue would thrust out and get in the way of his upper teeth and bottom lip when forming an F sound. He, in turn, would try to correct my disability. Needless to say, we accomplished nothing.

One can only imagine the comical situations in today's degraded language that a malady of this sort would bring to the surface. Especially since every other word uttered by the youth today seems to start with an F. However, even in that more innocent time, it still made for some unforgettable moments.

Every kid in class remembers Denny being dragged out of lunch line in school for some infraction. While the teacher was holding his ear, he'd turn to us all, gesture a goodbye, and blurt out, "So long, thellas!"

It didn't seem to embarrass him at all. We all thought he was hilarious. He laughed right along with everyone else. I admired him for that. If anyone laughed at me, my ears turned red and I would instantly black-ball the abuser as someone to ignore in the future.

The kids who mimicked me probably had no idea how much it hurt and embarrassed me. They couldn't have known it cut through my heart like a thunderbolt. Denny's problem, to me and everyone else, was funny, whereas mine was crippling and mortifying. We were all laughing with Denny, but those same kids could have been laughing at me. At least, that's the way I saw it.

---

Again, back to the boat: Big John, the owner, must have thought we made quite a pair, but he wanted to help. He led us to the smallest outboard engine I had ever seen. It was sitting in a 55-gallon drum filled with water. It didn't have a cover like most engines, maybe because it was built before they thought of enclosing them. He said it was old, but it worked perfectly. He even started it with his bare hands by spinning the flywheel without pulling the starter rope.

I was impressed and wanted it for our boat. The price was ten dollars. Denny and I talked it over and decided we needed to come back soon and get it. Of course, we never did.

We returned to our boat, and while attempting to figure out how to fix it, we tried to move it. Pieces of rotting wood were tearing apart in our hands. We looked at that decaying hull and the more we looked at it, the more the wishful dream became way too much for us to handle. There was so much mud in the bottom we couldn't turn it over. Though our best-laid plans had come to a halt, I still wanted a boat.

Later on that summer, I saw what looked like a boat for sale in the Sportsman store downtown. I call it a boat only because it had the same shape as one. In fact, it was probably a kid's play swimming pool, so in reality, the water was supposed to be inside this thing, but it was sold to me as a bona fide boat.

It was four feet long, two and one-half feet wide, and twelve inches high. It was made of a blue rubbery-plastic and cost only five dollars. Since I'd been mowing lawns for a couple of months, I had the money. After paying the man, I dragged it home. When I showed my purchase to Dad, he told me to take it back, that it was a total waste of five dollars, and it would never float with me in it. I was going to have to prove him wrong. Gritty determination set in.

In the basement, I began the task of transforming this fine craft into a sea-faring ship. First, I sat inside it. Space seemed a bit tighter than I expected, but it would have to make do. If I wanted any leg room, I would have to sit in the aft section.

After adjusting myself for comfort, I discovered there was no space in which to attach any kind of motor. I certainly wouldn't be able to pull a starter rope from this position and, of course, I had no money left over for one anyway. The options were oars, a paddle, or sail. I realized there was no way to attach the oar cleats to the side, and they would have to be tiny ones at best. I didn't have a paddle either, but I did have the makings for a sail.

I looked in the *World Book Encyclopedia* under sail boats to get an idea how the sail should look. Under schooners and cargo ships, I found the sails way too complicated and out of the question for my type of sailing. After all, I'd be cruising on a lake, not an ocean. Due to the constraints of my limited space, I decided a single mast in the middle would have to do. One with a square sail attached to it. I remembered seeing this type of rig in a Walt Disney movie.

How does one find the perfect mast? I searched the garage and found an old broom with a wooden handle. I surmised the mast should be about four feet tall, so I cut the handle to size. I would be questioned about Mom's ruined broom later. A looming problem became quite apparent; how to attach the mast to the bottom of the boat.

Cutting a hole through the bottom wasn't an option, but I thought about it. The only other idea was to tape it to the bottom using a relatively new product that Dad had on a nail above the workbench called duck tape. They changed the name of the stuff to duct tape when the color was changed from army green to a gray/silver, thus, matching the color of air ducts. I always referred to it as duck tape because it was easier to say. My mast was soon taped upright in the middle of the boat. I would have to straddle it, positioning my legs on either side. I didn't see a problem with that.

The mast was wobbly and needed to be supported by guy wires running from the perimeter of the boat to the top of the mast. This was tricky because I would need to leave enough room for me to come aboard. Nonetheless, I drilled some small holes into the flattened plastic that extruded from the top of the sides. I found some twine to use and first attached one piece each to the starboard and port sides. I ran it up to the top of the mast, then secured it with more duck tape.

I soon found out these two lines were woefully inadequate. I would need to repeat this process with more lines; two from each side of the stern and one from the bow. It was beginning to look more like a big spider web than a sea-going vessel, and I still needed to attach the sail.

I used part of an old sheet Mom let me have. I could tell she was enjoying my concentration on this project, because every time she checked my progress, she went back up the stairs chuckling.

How to attach the sail to the mast became the next dilemma to solve. I used to float small flat wooden boards in the street gutters after a good rain. For extra speed, a sail was improvised. I'd attach a pencil in a drilled hole in the wood, then skewered a playing card with two slits cut into it. This concept might work here as well. Since I was using a sheet instead of a sturdy playing card, I would need to add two cross members to my mast. I duck taped these on the sail.

I was finally finished. What a project this turned out to be, but it was all about to be worth it. I had my own boat ready for the big christening.

There was one thing for sure; my sailboat certainly didn't look store-bought. I climbed in to test it for practicality and ease of use. It completely failed on both counts. Sitting in the aft section, I couldn't see past the sail. I would have to lean over the sides to get any kind of view. My mobility was severely hampered by all the riggings. They rubbed my face and snapped my arms. In other words, it was perfect. Now off to the lake for its maiden voyage.

I hauled it up the basement stairs only to find out it was larger than the door opening. I had brought the project down by turning it sideways. Now the sail prevented me from doing that maneuver. I tried every angle, but no luck. I had to face the hard reality that I needed to dismember most of my rigging. I was beginning to wonder if Dad was right in his assessment. I went back down the stairs to tear apart all my good work.

Once the ship was dismantled and out of the basement, I reassembled the mass of sticks, twine, and tape in the garage. It looked almost as good as it had before. I wondered why I hadn't built it in the garage in the first place.

I managed to drag it down to the highway that led to Big Spirit Lake. Once there, I stuck out my thumb and waited for someone to stop and take me and my sailboat to the water.

Eventually, someone with a truck couldn't resist stopping for what must have been the saddest looking salty dog he'd ever seen. He dropped me off at the beach with a hearty, "YO HO!"

Over the sand and down to the water's edge I went. Finally! Now I was ready for the big moment.

Once in the water, my boat was quite unsteady when any amount of weight was put on the bottom. I brought it out to the water's edge and carefully climbed in as I had practiced in the basement. I tried to slide my way into the water by several scooching maneuvers, paddling with my arms in the sand like a sea turtle when she's going to lay her eggs. It didn't budge an inch. I would have to enter the craft while it was afloat.

I took it out only a few feet to where the water was maybe a foot deep. Holding on to the mast, I lifted my right leg over the side and attempted to climb in. My vessel would have none of it. It slipped out of my grip, and over the top of the mast I flipped with my leg tangling in the lines. When I pulled myself out of the water, I looked woefully at what was left of my dream voyager.

There would be no sailing this boat again. I was frustrated and embarrassed. The beach was crowded with people. I surmised all of them were watching my every move from the time I dragged this crappy blue tub down to the waterline. I was not going to look up to confirm it. I tore out all the riggings, the twine, the tape, and the broomstick and threw them onto the sand in a tangled stupid pile.

This was about the time I noticed there was no wind at all; the air was dead calm. My boat never had a chance.

Okay, I thought, maybe I could find a paddle somewhere and salvage my five dollar investment. With all that sail crap out of my way, maybe I could turn it into a short canoe. I pulled it behind me while I swam out a bit further. Without the sail, now maybe I would be able to see where I was going and actually navigate this thing. Also, I didn't need to be as careful when attempting to come aboard.

I leaped headfirst over the transom and into the bottom of my now new and improved paddle boat. I turned myself around and sat upright.

Water immediately rushed in over the sides. I tried sitting aft, but water then rushed in over the transom. Not having any inclination to bale, I let her sink with me in it. If I had been able to breathe down there, I would have stayed sitting on the bottom of the lake in the crappy tub until everyone had left the beach. The crowd must have been howling by now.

I swam to shore and walked back to the road, leaving my blue goose at the bottom of the lake. It was now fulfilling its rightful destiny; the miserable thing finally had water in it.

# CHAPTER NINE

# LLOYD AND ME

A few years after the blue boat fiasco, my brother Mike obtained some SCUBA gear (self-contained underwater breathing apparatus). The outfit consisted of an old air tank, a weight belt, fins, mask, snorkel, regulator, and a black quarter-inch thick wetsuit.

The wetsuit came with a hood, a two-piece body suit, gloves, and boots. Unlike today, this suit didn't come with zippers, Velcro straps, or interior lining for easy dressing. And unlike today, it wasn't made of neoprene, but some kind of sponge-rubber.

Mike and his friend Chuck Finley would go diving in golf course lakes to retrieve balls or in the Okoboji lakes where fisherman were known to snag their fishing lures and lose them.

Buffalo Run, located on Big Spirit Lake, had a spot where Mike sank an old bedspring offshore to ensure success while lure hunting. It's probably still there. Once hooked on that thing, any three dollar fish lure was a goner. Mike came home with all kinds of stories of their exploits and boxes full of rusty fishing tackle.

*Sea Hunt* was a popular TV show at that time, starring Lloyd Bridges. Every week he was fighting bad guys underwater with the aid of scuba gear. It was always pretty exciting stuff, and the winner was usually decided by who cut whose air hose first.

I was already intrigued with the sport even though it was relatively new. In my mind, it was ultra-cool to be associated with anything that had to do with scuba diving. For some reason only known to the gods, my brother Mike let me take all his gear to the lake by myself and give it a try. I could not believe my good fortune.

The night before my dive, I laid all the gear out on the floor of our room with the suit spread out flat, complete with the hood, gloves, and boots. I put the weight belt on the waist, the mask and snorkel on the hood, and the fins on the boots. It was most impressive, and exactly how I remembered Lloyd doing it on *Sea Hunt*. This way it was easy to spot anything missing.

Everything was good to go. The tank had enough air for at least an hour of deep diving. Mike showed me how to mount the regulator on the air tank and how to breathe with it. He also mentioned that if I would be diving in Big Spirit Lake, I should leave the wetsuit home because the water would be nearly eighty-five degrees, and I wouldn't need it. I told him that I might take his advice, but I wasn't sure yet.

He'd be at work when I left for the lake so it would be my call. I chose to have the whole scuba diving experience, the entire spectacle. I wanted to be the man in *Sea Hunt*. I was about to do the ultimate coolest thing, to be the utmost amazing guy. I was going to a crowded beach to scuba dive in full view of everyone. All the people out there would be watching, wishing they could be me. It was almost like Lloyd Bridges and I were buddies. I would wait until the hottest part of the day, to run into the biggest adoring crowd. I was finally going to be the lucky stiff, and I would not be ruining it by having to talk.

---

First, some lawns needed to be mowed in the morning. It would help keep my mind off scuba diving for a few hours. I had about six regular mowing accounts and, depending on the rain, I would mow them every week or two. Hurrying through the work most of the time, I didn't see the big picture or importance of a well-maintained lawn. I'd only cut the grass, not rake up the clippings afterward, and my mower certainly didn't have a bag attachment. I'd seen those baggers around on some of the more expensive big mowers and wondered why people would mess with clippings if they didn't have to.

The Kentucky bluegrass that grows in Iowa doesn't need a border to trim like Bermuda grass does in the South, so lawn care to me was just mowing as fast as I could race around the yard.

Every other kid in town used his dad's mower. I was no different. It was a small eighteen-inch-wide machine with a three-horsepower

Briggs and Stratton engine. It was showing its age after years of abuse from me. One day Dad came home with a brand new self-propelled, twenty-one-inch mower with a four-horsepower engine.

I helped him unload it from the back of his Desoto station wagon and said, "W-w-what a n-nice l-l-lawn m-m-mower, Dad."

"It sure is. It was fifty bucks, and you're going to pay for it," he informed me.

He handed me my first payment book. I was to pay the hardware store $7.50 a month for eight months. I was leery of all this, but I had little choice in the matter. Being a debtor now, I had officially become more of a businessman than just a kid with his Dad's lawnmower. Despite the intimidation of a monthly payment, I was excited to try this thing out; after all, it was self-propelled.

I hated making my first payment; seven dollars and fifty cents gone. I hated my second payment even more. By the time the fourth one came around, it was autumn, and all lawn mowing had stopped. I was raking leaves, but not enough to save up the seven-fifty. The coupon book was in my dresser drawer reminding me every day that I was screwed. Before too long I was begging Mom to help me pay this thing off. Guess I was going back to being just a kid with his dad's lawnmower again.

Once when I finished mowing Mrs. McFarland's yard, I decided to leave the engine on while I walked home since the self-propelled action only worked while it was running. It was easier than pushing it cold.

Dale Simmonds lived next door to us and had a beautiful lawn. That day, for some reason, I walked across his lawn, cutting a pathway as I went. I could have stayed on the sidewalk, but with all the dust blowing up, I chose to use his lawn as my detour.

Sometimes I did stupid things like that; not out of malice or spitefulness, just oblivious as to the consequences. I was surprised when he knocked on our door and asked if I had just cut a path across his lawn. Dale was an easy-going, funny man; the sort of good neighbor everyone wants.

I accompanied him to have a look at what I had done. There it was, a twenty-one-inch swath cut in his otherwise perfect yard. How stupid! He laughed about that incident the rest of his life, always bringing it up whenever I made it back home for a visit.

One night the Simmonds' planned something to return the favor. Dale, his wife, and daughter decided to walk into our house through the front door and across our living room where all six of our family members were watching television. They walked between us and the TV set, one at a time, then out the back door. Absolutely no one in our family noticed. They called when they got home and told us what they had just done. It, too, was a standing joke forever.

Our yard was certainly not anything to be proud of. It was a place where everyone in the neighborhood played; the grass was a secondary afterthought. Dad didn't seem to be concerned, so no one else was either.

The best yard in our neighborhood was owned by Mr. Thorton. His house was set far back, allowing him to showcase his lawn. I believe he may have had an underground sprinkler system long before they became commonplace. His lawn was mowed level; it was always green, with no dry spots. We were never allowed to walk on it, which made him the grouch of the block. He would never allow a lawn-hack like me to go near his place with a mower. Since earning a B.S. degree in Landscape Architecture over forty years ago, I've totally turned into that man.

———————————

It was almost noon and my mowing jobs were finished. I went home and rolled the mower into its spot in the garage, never once removing the caked-on dried grass off the undercarriage. I gathered all the scuba gear, packing the wetsuit into a milk crate along with the mask, fins, snorkel, and the regulator on top.

It was heavy and, with the weight of the tank, which I would have to carry on my back, I decided the twenty-pound weight belt was unnecessary and would leave it home. With all this stuff in the crate plus the air tank, why would I need any more weight? I was finally ready. It was showtime.

The highway that led to Big Spirit Lake was only a block away, downhill, but by the time I got there, I was hot, sweaty, and exhausted. I put out my thumb until someone stopped.

Once at the public beach, I found a place where I would be surrounded by lots of sunbathers and began the process of impressing them. The sand was hot, so I put the booties on first. I attached the regulator to the tank and turned on the air valve. I tested the system by breathing as loud as I could into the mouthpiece to get the attention of anyone who might have missed my entrance. It was time to pull the bodysuit pants on. I was sweating profusely. I pulled and pulled and grunted and tugged. My hands were soon tired and cramping. Once the pants were pulled up around my legs, I struggled to get them up to my waist. There! Now for the jacket.

It was even more difficult. Only one arm could be used to get the other one into the sleeve. I was hopping and jumping around trying anything I could to get this thing in place. The audience must have been having a good time rubbernecking my performance. By the time the jacket was on, I was experiencing symptoms of heat stroke.

I was dressed in a black sponge rubber suit that had no evaporative relief qualities whatsoever, standing on hot sand in the sun. My head was pounding. I began to feel faint and weak. I still had to pull that beavertail strap attached to the back of the jacket up between my legs and attach it to the front of the coat with two turn-clasps. I was too weak to accomplish this task, so I let it dangle around the back of my knees. I was already settling for a notch below ultra-coolness.

My hands were beginning to shake, so I sat in the sand to catch my breath, which was impossible to do because of the suit's squeeze effect that was restricting my breathing. This was a common drawback associated with those old quarter-inch sponge rubber suits which would compress the chest cavity especially at depth or deep diving. I began hyperventilating when someone next to me asked if I was going to be all right. "Ya," I lied, "I d-d-do this all the t-t-time."

I was also too weak to pull the hood over my head, and there was no chance I was going to wear the gloves. Somehow I managed to get the tank onto my back, the regulator into my mouth, and my fins onto my feet. I backed my way down to the water's edge like I'd seen Lloyd do several times. All the while hoping I wouldn't trip and fall because there was no way I could ever get up again by myself.

At this point, I didn't give a hoot who was watching and who was laughing. All I wanted was to splash into the water before I passed out.

Once in the lake, I observed people of all ages, some with their babies splashing around having a grand old time in the warm water with nothing on but swimming suits. There I was, dressed for arctic diving.

I finally splashed into the water and obtained some much-needed relief from the heat. I adjusted my mask after spitting in it like I saw Lloyd do every week and swam further out to the deeper water.

While swimming out, I noticed I wasn't sinking. I was totally buoyant. The gear hadn't come with a BCD or buoyancy control device, so if I wasn't sinking now, I was not going to be later. I guessed that's what the weight belt was for. I tried to submerge myself with what little strength I had left by breast-stroking downward. My butt was popping up to the surface like a big black bobber with my legs flailing around and completely useless. My Bozo-like fins only accentuated the sorry spectacle.

What humiliation. Some of those same people on the beach could very well have witnessed my sinking in the five-dollar blue boat. What a revolting development this was. Now I was trying to sink and I couldn't.

A wetsuit is designed to trap a thin layer of water between the skin and the suit, which reaches body temperature quickly. This keeps the diver warm in cold water. However, in ninety-degree water, and on an already sweaty person, it matches the body temperature and creates too much heat. Especially if the diver is flapping his appendages and desperately attempting to get to the bottom. I was overheating again with no relief forthcoming.

I didn't care anymore about diving, looking cool, or Lloyd Bridges. The water was so green I could barely see my hand in front of my face. Even if the visibility had been a hundred feet and I, somehow, managed to stay on the bottom, there was absolutely nothing to see but sand on the lake floor. No sunken treasure, no dazzling fish, nothing, and I still had to lug this crap home.

I made my way to shore and ripped off the tank and suit as fast as I possibly could. Removing a wetsuit is a lot like peeling a banana; it's ten times easier than pulling it on, so it was accomplished in short order. I dove into the water and floated face down for fifteen minutes, using my snorkel to breathe and allowed my body to cool back to a suitable temperature. Regaining strength, and any self-respect I could muster, I packed the gear, walked out to the road, and thumbed a ride home. Sorry Lloyd, I let you down.

# CHAPTER TEN

# WHAT'S A FATHER TO DO?

My father came home after WWII like millions of other young men looking for mainly two things; someone to marry and a job, and not particularly in that order. His generation had lived through the Great Depression, fought and won a mother of a war, and witnessed our nation gain superpower status in the world, effectively taking over Great Britain's top spot. Everything was looking up for the young people who survived the war, and it was time to get on with living.

My dad's version of getting on with living would bring him back to his hometown of Gillette Grove. He told us he had graduated in the top ten of his high school class, then finished the statement by confessing there were only eight other kids in it. His father owned the only general store in that tiny town, and Dad went back to work for him.

Just before Dad was shipped by the Army overseas to Italy and North Africa, he was stationed on the Northwest coast. While there, he went on a blind date with Hazel Lee Edelen. She was just out of high school and a welder in the wartime shipyards, aka; "Rosie the Riveter." She and her family had just moved from the St. Louis area of Missouri, where she grew up. Somehow he convinced her to come back to Iowa after the war ended and marry him. This happened in September of 1945. She was nineteen, and he was twenty-three.

They lived in an old home next to his parents; a home with an outhouse instead of an indoor toilet. My mother was about to be inundated by all of my Dad's family; his parents next door and four of his siblings within ten miles. She had left a relatively good life near the beaches of Washington State to live in a town without sidewalks or a traffic light, and a house that required mukluks to use the bathroom in winter.

My brother Mike was born eleven months later, and by the time I arrived on the scene two years after that, she felt the pressures of her new life closing in on her. She was up to her neck in kids, Andersens, and outhouses. I'm sure Dad was feeling the pressures of parenthood and financial responsibilities as well. To make matters worse, he was plagued with migraine headaches as I would be later on, starting in my twenties.

It seems my Dad and I struggled from the get-go. Once, on a Christmas day in Gillette Grove at Grandma's house, all the cousins and their Dads were outside sledding down the biggest hill I'd ever seen. Everyone was having a grand time on this wonderful snowy day in Iowa. Once down the quarter-mile snow-packed gravel road, one of the uncles would drive the kids back up for another run. It was a perfect day for family fun.

I was almost four and, unfortunately, afraid I wouldn't be able to steer my sled or stop if need be, so I chose to sit on it and watch. Dad wanted me to participate, but I wouldn't. He became increasingly frustrated and eventually put me in a bedroom alone to think about it while my cousins were outside having so much fun. I could see from the window how excited they were while I was alone on the bed with nothing to do but think about it.

Grandma kept her extra Christmas tree light bulbs in a box in this room and, while there, I found one. As always with small children, it ended up in my mouth. Unfortunately, I couldn't get it out again, having struggled to push it in. My muffled cry for help eventually brought Dad to my rescue. The crying was preventing my mouth from opening wide enough for him to get a grip on the threaded end of the bulb. I must have bitten down while his finger was in my mouth because that's when the real frustration of the whole sledding incident exploded.

His temper was frightening me, and before it was over, I bit down on the glass bulb and it shattered in my mouth. My tongue started bleeding. I was howling now, which brought in Mom and a few aunts, but Dad was not about to throw in the towel. I had spoiled his day and I had spoiled my day. He rinsed my mouth out in the sink in the freezing bathroom, brought me back into the bedroom and made me think about it some more.

It was over. All he wanted was for his son to experience a thrilling sled ride down that hill. He just wanted me to join his brothers' kids in having a grand time. I wish I had been man enough.

In 1952, there was a big flood in Sioux City and the Missouri River crested at twenty-four feet above its banks. The levees burst and major damage occurred in that rather large city. Dad drove us all down to see it in the station wagon.

I was three and only remember standing with a lot of strangers behind a wrought iron fence. We were on top of a 200-foot cliff overlooking the vast panoramic view below. There was lots of water and bridges stranded in the middle of it all. Of course, I had no idea what was happening or what we were supposed to be looking at. I began stomping my feet on the turf around the fence while avoiding a lot of big people's knees to pass the time. Eventually, I stepped into an area where the dirt was eroding beneath the fence, when all of a sudden a large chunk of earth gave way and down I went. I remember grabbing the cross member at the bottom of the fence. The shoe on my left foot slipped off and fell the 200 feet to the bottom of the cliff.

There were screams and great commotion. The next thing I realized, Dad had reached down, grabbed my wrist and yanked me back up through the hole. It all happened quickly. I soon started reacting fearfully to all the hubbub and the look on Mom's face. But mostly to Dad's anger, which was probably brought on by relief and maybe some embarrassment. After all, he had let me out of his sight in a dangerous place, and he probably sensed the disapproval of the bystanders gathered around. He sat me down hard on a park bench in the back of the crowd with instructions not to move again until we left. Mom sat with me and made sure I didn't. I guess Mom and I were both supposed to think about it.

Embarrassed or not, he'd just saved his little boy's life.

As with most kids, I spent an inordinate amount of time attempting to stay within the limits of my dad's good graces. Every decision I made, every idea I might act upon usually resulted in gaining the approval or, most likely, the disapproval of his all-seeing eye. Kids, by and large, fail to heed the still, small voice urging them to rethink what they are about to do.

One year the Christmas tree lighting cord was plugged into an overloaded outlet. Mike and I accidently discovered that by plugging the lights into the socket (as we used to call them), electricity would arc and scare the daylights out of any unsuspecting sap. We decided to pull a prank on my poor little six-year-old sister, Marcia. We bet her that she wasn't smart enough to plug in the Christmas lights all by herself. As she was attempting to do just that, Mike and I were watching and holding back our tell-tale snickers when our plan went awry. The arc was much bigger than we had previously seen. It made a loud pop and blackened her whole hand.

Off she went, screaming and crying to Mom. We both felt rotten about what we had done to her. She was such a sweet little girl, always a peacemaker. Mom came running to us asking how in the world we could have been so cruel. We were to stay in our rooms and wait for Dad to get home.

Every kid hated that. The wait was always much worse than the actual punishment; at least it had been until now. We weren't so sure this time.

We passed the hours blaming each other, but only one thing was forefront in our minds. At six o'clock, Dad would be returning home from work, and Mom would be giving him one more job to do.

We were lucky this happened when Dad was working in town. Sometimes he was on the road all week. If one of our infractions occurred on a Monday and he was out of town, we'd have five whole days to await the penalty. The joys of childhood would have to sit that week out because anything fun would have been overshadowed by the impending doom coming to us on Friday night.

Poor Dad would sometimes complain about always having to be the bad guy. He was always the one expected to dole out the corporal punishment when maybe he wanted Mom to take some of the slack. She never did; it just wasn't in her nature.

Mike and I were lying on our twin beds. We heard him drive up and park. We heard the screen door slam as he entered the kitchen. There was talking back and forth. We assumed he was inspecting Marcia's little hand by now. The gallows walk began up the stairs to our prison room. He opened the door and looked at us.

He then had us both lie on one of the beds. We were already crying, hoping our remorse might temper his anger. Strangely enough, this time he didn't display the usual frustration we had come to expect in a situation like this. His heart didn't seem to be in it. He took off his belt like we'd seen him do before, and our eyes opened wide with terror.

The belt-strapping was more mental than anything else. We were fully clothed, and he was hardly applying any real force with his blows; however, we still kicked and writhed as if we were being ruthlessly horse-whipped. It was all over in fifteen seconds. When he left, Mike and I looked at each other and shrugged. Was that all we're going to get?

I guess it was, because Mom called us down for dinner. That's the last time his belt was used on us, but he still made the grabbing the belt buckle gesture whenever he wanted our complete attention. It worked every time.

Mike was a pretty good kid, compliant, always wanting to please Dad. I was not like Mike. Dad was always having to deal with me and the ridiculous stunts I pulled, as he would refer to them. I have to admit, I gave him plenty of ammunition.

Case in point: We never owned expensive furniture when I was growing up. Most families I knew didn't either, so it was no big deal. The nicest piece my mother owned was a mahogany buffet that adorned our dining room area, adjacent to the kitchen. We always ate at the kitchen table next to the stove and refrigerator. The dining room was saved for rare sit-down dinners with guests using our good plate ware instead of the puke-colored Melmac we used every day. Needless to say, the dining room was seldom used. Truthfully, I don't remember using it one time for dinner. It was more a crafts room. Mom would use it as a sewing space, Mike built several model airplanes and I assembled model plastic cars in there. Mom kept the lace tablecloth and the good silverware inside the buffet along with a couple of large bowls and her pretty candlesticks.

One uneventful day, I discovered that I could make scrape marks through the varnished finish on top of Mom's treasured buffet with a coin. I had the power to ruin something, not unlike discovering the power to bend a metal fork for the first time. I had no clue I was doing something that may lead to unpleasantness.

I carefully scraped my name, "Doug." I was quite proud of my accomplishment. Much to my surprise and dismay, when Mom saw it, she was disheartened and asked, "What in the world were you thinking when you did this?"

Wondering what I did that was so wrong, I offered the only explanation I could, considering the situation, "M-Marcia d-d-did it!"

Well, rats! That response earned me a trip to my room-prison and one more long wait for Dad to get home.

When he finally did, he called me down so we could both inspect my handiwork. I confessed it wasn't my sister who did this, but me.

This confession came after many attempts at thwarting the truth. About the only person I didn't accuse was him. Up the gallows stairs and into the bedroom we went. He said this spanking I was about to receive wasn't for the stupid act of vandalism, but for lying afterward.

He also recited the much-used spanking preamble, "This is going to hurt me more than it will you."

He actually said those words. Maybe some other kid would buy it, but I didn't. It was, however, my last spanking. I had graduated to the next level; groundings.

Some of my antics didn't involve pranks or minor destructiveness, but instead an element of real danger entered into the picture.

The Town of Spirit Lake built a big new water tower by the high school. It was huge compared to the old one downtown near the police station. My friend, Tim Peters, and I discovered one day that the perimeter security gate in the fencing surrounding the tower was unlocked. We also saw that the maintenance ladder which began on the ground level and extended up to the platform encircling the massive tank resulted in direct access for a kid. Instead of seeing this as a design flaw of major proportions, we viewed it as a stroke of good luck. I'd never been on anything higher than my house. That was about to change.

We climbed the steel rungs, looking down only a couple of times before deciding it was better to concentrate on where we were going instead of where we had been. When the two of us finally reached the platform, we found another ladder leading to the very top of the tank, which we also climbed. Once on top, we were amazed at the size of this giant aqua blue water tank. The surface was so vast and relatively flat that we could run around on it without feeling like we were in any real danger.

The view was stunning and, in a way, educational. Looking north, I could see Big Spirit Lake, the whole lake, and beyond that, the State of Minnesota. Imagine that; I could actually see a different state from where I was standing. To the east and south, I saw East Okoboji Lake wrapping around the town and surrounding farmlands. There was the Town of Milford, eight miles south. Westward, the popular Arnolds Park, and West Okoboji Lake were spread out like a map. It was all so inspiring and beautiful.

Okoboji maps were sold to tourists everywhere, but to see the actual layout from this elevation was to finally understand the whole area in a new perspective. I decided I would have to return often.

I spotted my house and my friends' houses. I located the beach where I'd sunk my stupid blue boat. I saw the railroad tracks where we walked with our BB guns, the church I attended on Sundays, and the lawns I mowed spread all over town.

I now understood why people on the ground were described as looking like ants when viewed from great heights. All the hustle and bustle of cars darting here and there was captivating to me. I could see them, but not hear them.

I locked in on one car that looked like it was moving closer to our position. Wait a minute! I knew that one; it was one of the two police cars in town. Maybe this was just a coincidence that the police were coming our way. The squad car might turn away at the next street. Okay, maybe the next one. How about the one after this one?

Perhaps he didn't see us. Tim and I dropped to our stomachs on the flat tank top, not moving, holding our breath. In a couple of minutes, I garnered enough courage to slowly peek over the edge. The patrol car was parked directly below.

Oh, crap! I'd never been in real trouble before, not with the law. This wasn't like forgetting my chores or slamming the screen door when Dad was asleep on the sofa with a headache, or even electrocuting my sister's hand; this was serious.

There would be no escape from an officer with a real gun. What was Dad going to do? I couldn't think about that now, as I had to retain some semblance of dignity when dealing with the law in the presence of my friend Tim. I immediately started crying. Tim, to his credit, looked at me with great anguish, but he didn't give in to emotion. I've always admired him for that.

The officer yelled, "You two kids come down from there immediately!"

Tim and I looked at each other. Who, us? Was he talking to us?

We began our descent. Once down, we put our bikes into the trunk of the patrol car and were given a ride to the station. When we arrived, he called our parents to come and get us.

Man alive. Now Dad had to collect his son at the jail house. This was just a step below the reform school for boys at Eldora, which was just a step below the state slammer in Madison.

Was I a felon now? Was I going to have to be associated with a lot of people with bad teeth? I couldn't believe this was happening. The day started out so well. Please, God, make this all a horrible dream.

The officer showed us what a jail cell looked like and explained to us how stupid this stunt was. Tim's dad came within five minutes. I was left waiting for over an hour. My dad had decided to let me learn a lesson by staying down there for an extended period of time to let me think about it, again.

Finally, not being paid to be a babysitter, the officer loaded me and my bike back into his car and took me home. I slouched down in the front seat, embarrassed to be seen in a black and white like a common criminal.

At home, I had to face Dad, and I was braced for just about anything except for what happened.

Luckily, my parents had company over. Dad loved entertaining people as he was quite a gregarious guy. It always put him in a good mood. Probably the extra hour he gave me at the police station worked in my favor and gave him time to simmer down. Between that and the company, there was no yelling, just instructions for the two-week grounding period about to commence. He even let me out on parole the next day when all the cousins came to visit.

Maybe he was pleased that I finally showed some death-defying spunk. No matter what the reason, no one was more surprised than I.

---

Dad and I seldom talked about my stuttering in any constructive way. Mostly we ignored the obvious. It was the elephant in the room no one wanted to mention. Neither of us knew how to correct the situation, so what was there to talk about? Whatever the reason for his attitude, I don't believe he was aware how seriously it was affecting my everyday life or how it was going to shape my future.

He was my most difficult person to talk to. We seldom had discussions about anything other than why I had just pulled my latest stunt. For me, it was normally a defensive conversation, having only a short window of time to state my case before he would throw up his hands in disgust and walk away.

Defending my reasons for doing whatever I did in a current situation caused stress, which brought about more disfluency, usually with a vengeance. He was uncomfortable standing there while I experienced blocks in my speech.

Blocks are much worse than the standard repetition of a sound like p-p-p-purple. At least with the repetition, the word is eventually said, but with a blockage, it may never come out. Add to that the facial contortions, which could be most unnerving, I would think, to the listener. A blockage was the result of a struggling effort to squeeze a word out of my clenched lips or around a tongue with a mind of its own.

Usually, a word with a hard onset, (which I discuss later), such as clever, gutter, justice or lettuce would trigger these deeply humiliating situations. My jaw would tremble uncontrollably for a period of time. My lips would struggle to open to the point that a crowbar might be required to help loosen them again. My tongue might be lifted up to the roof of my mouth with extreme pressure. My eyes would blink uncontrollably, and my ears would almost cease to function.

By the time any semblance of the attempted word might make its way out of my contortionist's mouth, I could see the squirming I was causing anyone in earshot. All this pointed to one outcome; dismal failure. I was continually petrified about my obtaining any sort of success in my future. This perpetual nightmare can be debilitating. Every stutterer deals with it in their own way, usually by trial and error. If something works for a while to lessen the problem, use it. But, as I stated earlier, eventually every word becomes the hard word to say.

Since I never had the opportunity, or the inclination, to see my face when a blockage occurred, I can only imagine Dad's sadness and frustration in his inability to do anything about it.

He probably worried about me and my future much more than I knew. I know now it must have weighed heavily on his mind. I hope he never blamed himself for my problem because I didn't. I regret we struggled in our ability to simply talk to each other. Most people found Dad to be a kind, outgoing, funny man. Again, I missed out on that part. With me, he had to be just Dad.

---

One time my parents tried to take the bull by the horns and tackle this stuttering curse head-on. We had some good friends, the Williams, whose daughter, Becky, had developed a kind of tic. She'd be walking along and for no reason, kick out her leg; a sort of mini-Tourette's syndrome. It looked like she had just stepped into a pile of dog doo and was trying to shake it off. The Williams had her treated by a hypnotist in a neighboring town, curing her almost instantly.

Dad, Mom, and I went to see this man one night. It would be the lone constructive attempt at doing something professional with my defect. Up to that point in my life, I had heard at least once if not several times:

- Slow down!
- Think before you speak!
- Take a deep breath first.
- Try saying it with marbles in your mouth.
- Relax your tongue.
- No one else in our family does it.
- You don't stutter when you sing.
- Watch me. See how I do it.
- Repeat saying, Walla Walla, Washington three times (my personal favorite).

These oft-heard suggestions of well-intentioned folks weren't helping, so we set up an appointment with Doctor Whitlock. I doubt he was an actual doctor of any kind. He was a short man with an enormous girth and could have easily played the part of Mayor of Munchkinland.

Upon arriving, my parents, the good doctor, his wife, and I sat around in his living room for about half an hour and chatted uncomfortably. I knew I was on the preverbal spot, so my speech was worse than usual. I was too embarrassed to talk about it, even with someone my parents were hiring to fix it. I frowned on anything or anyone who brought attention to it.

———————

To illustrate this point, a cousin of mine once told me a joke he had heard at school. It seems that two fellows with parachutes were about to jump out of a burning airplane.

The one who stuttered asked the other, "How d-d-do I know w-w-w-when t-t-to p-p-pull the r-r-ripcord?"

The man told him to count to ten, then pull it.

They both jumped and the stutterer started counting, "One, t-t-two, th-th-three, f-f-four, SPLAT!"

My cousin, trying to control his laughter, exclaimed, "That guy sounds just like you, just like you!"

By this time my ears had turned red and, I couldn't hear him anymore. He hadn't intended to hurt or embarrass me, he just thought I would find this particular joke funny because I could relate to it better than most. He had no idea how much pain, mortification, and frustration I went through every waking hour of every day. I always found it curious that people didn't know how incredibly sensitive to it I was. I wanted Porky Pig to end up in a ham and cheese sandwich.

---

Anyway, here I was, sitting there on the sofa thinking, "So please, Doctor, everyone, just fix my nightmare; let's get on with the program."

I'd seen a hypnotist do a show once at the school's auditorium. This guy had the whole place in stitches. Those under his influence were popping up like Whack-a-Moles yelling at the top of their lungs phrases like "Viva la France!" and "Long live the Queen!"

I had confidence that this might work for me. I even lived next door to the huge kid who insisted for thirty minutes during the show that his name was Mary while being under this entertainer's spell.

When Dad told me I was going to be cured by hypnosis, I wanted it to work more than I'd ever wanted anything. This would be life-changing, and we all knew it.

No one more than me.

The ride to his town had been excruciatingly slow. The small talk in the living room was unnecessary. Let's get on with the business of why I'm here. Make it all just go away, please, Dr. Whitlock.

Please, God, help him make this work for me.

The doctor and I eventually went into his office where he began preparing me for my session. I sat on a chair on one side of the room, and he sat across from me against a wall. It was actually his bedroom as opposed to an office. It could have been an outhouse in August for all I cared, just fix me.

He explained what hypnotism was and that it was safe and totally harmless. He had a spot on the wall above his head almost to the ceiling and instructed me not to take my eyes off it and relax. I didn't know how to relax, so I waited for more instructions.

I was to concentrate on the spot, and I would be feeling myself becoming drowsy, my eyelids becoming heavy, and my arms were turning into sacks of flour. I was waiting for this sensation to begin.

After the third suggestion that I absolutely couldn't keep my eyes open, I decided to speed up the process and see if he had anything else in his bag of tricks. I still wanted this to work, so I closed my eyes.

He made suggestions about how my tongue would relax and how I might organize my thoughts before I began the process of speech. He said I would remember to take deep breaths between sentences and this would, in turn, slow me down into a comfortable, relaxed rhythm. At this point, I was waiting for him to mention Walla Walla and marbles.

He suggested some other clean up duties concerning bed wetting and not being a class clown. I guess my folks were trying to get their money's worth; three for the price of one.

The session lasted about thirty minutes, and at the end, he added a little sideshow for the folks. He told me whenever he put his hand on my shoulder that I would become thirsty.

I didn't want to have to go through this charade anymore. I was disappointed and I wanted out. Nothing had changed.

He brought me out of my faux-hypnotic state, and we joined my parents and his wife in the living room. I don't know what everyone was expecting, but I just wanted to go home.

We continued our chit chat, and after a short while, he came over to where I was sitting, wanting to prove to everyone that he had succeeded in our first session. I dreaded this.

He laid his hand on my shoulder. Nothing. I knew I was supposed to suddenly blurt out how thirsty I was, but it all seemed so silly. He leaned on my shoulder with more force.

I figured a white lie beats a broken clavicle, so I said, "B-b-boy! I'm as thirsty as they c-c-come!"

He showed me where the cups were in the kitchen, and he returned to the others to explain what had just happened. After dumping the entire glass of water down the sink, I joined them again and faked a yawn. For me, it was time to go.

Once in the car, I told Mom and Dad what I had done, that I was fully awake and aware during the entire process and I had faked it so as not to cause him any embarrassment. They were disappointed my stuttering wasn't going to be brushed away by some fat man's magic.

I was going to have to somehow deal with this on my own. We never went back. It may have worked for Becky's kicking leg, but stuttering proved to be much more of a challenge. Hypnotism was no match for what ailed me. I hope Dad stopped the check.

**My Dad, Ernest (Sam) Andersen (far right),
with four of his five siblings.
Circa 1943**

**The Sioux City Flood of 1952.
The location where I slipped under the iron fence.**

# CHAPTER ELEVEN

# HOLLYWOOD, GUNS, AND GOD

Summer thunderstorms in Iowa are fairly frequent, and a lot of rain can fall in a short period of time. Most occur in the evening. One particular night the rain that fell was warm, and it accumulated on the ground rapidly. This meant only one thing to all the kids in our neighborhood: worms.

Another name for the earthworms that live in the soil in the Midwest is night crawlers. During heavy rain, they come out of the ground and expose themselves on the surface for at least two reasons; to prevent drowning and to mate.

This night there were over fifteen of us kids running around with flashlights gathering worms like manna on the Sinai Peninsula. We'd never seen so many before. Some of us loaded them into Folger's coffee cans; others filled their hands with masses of the squirming slimy, mucus-oozing creatures hanging between their fingers. Some of their bounties fell back to the ground as they ran to the central depositing area; our yard.

The worms were dumped off and the kids would run and gather their next load. This went on for over an hour. We ended up with at least twenty gallons of writhing worms. Some of the kids took a dozen worms or so home with them, but most were left with my brother and me.

Night crawlers are the bait of choice when fishing in the Okoboji area. Bullheads, catfish, perch, walleye, northern and Muskie-pike all gobble them up. After a rain such as we just had, "Night Crawlers for

Sale" signs suddenly appeared all over town posted on the elm trees that lined every street.

That was before the dreaded Dutch elm disease killed every single American elm in Iowa in a matter of just a few years. It was a tragedy watched in slow motion. Elms were the perfect tree for street planting with their arching shape that would form a tunnel when the branches on one side of the street met the branches from the other side. For that reason, every town in Iowa had planted thousands of them. For three seasons out of the year, they were a sight to behold. In winter, shed of their leaves, the remaining skeletons were just another depressing reminder of the seemingly endless cold and sunless days.

Mike and I didn't know how to preserve that many worms. Ideally, we would have packaged them in separate containers of one dozen each, using peat moss as filler and refrigerated them, but who had peat moss, containers, or an empty fridge? We dumped all twenty gallons of them in a couple of wooden boxes, added regular dirt and some of Mom's used coffee grounds as the magic preserver. We'd heard about that somewhere, probably Mom, who wanted to get rid of some coffee grounds.

Business was slow. As the days went by, the prices dropped all over town from twenty-five cents to fifteen cents a dozen. This meant everyone's worms were beginning to rot where they lay. At least ours were. It was not an easy task to sell supposedly fresh, plump, night crawlers to an angler who had to hold his nose while I dug around the worm graveyard in search of twelve that somehow managed to survive. I'd finally pull one out and jiggle my hand to mimic some form of life.

"S-s-see? This one seems to be r-r-real l-l-lively!"

After a few days, we had over a thousand dead smelly worms to bury again. Sort of returning them from whence they came. This was the reason Dad asked me the day after we captured them what I was going to do with twenty gallons of worms.

"S-s-s-sell them," I answered.

"Why don't you call Bob down at the bait store by the bridge and see if he needs any?" he asked. "That way you wouldn't have to store them."

I was petrified. Did he want me to actually call a real live businessman and ask if he would like to purchase something from a no-account boy? Did he forget about my problem? Either he insisted, or I agreed, but in any event, we went up the stairs to his bedroom to make the call.

Dad sat on the bed and watched me pick up the phone after looking up the bait shop's number in the phone book. He had a slight grin, but very much wanted this venture to work out for me.

"Number, please," the operator asked.

"N-n-nine, f-f-four, t-t-two, eight please," I managed to squeeze out.

I was about to talk to a stranger, an adult stranger, about the remote possibility of him purchasing worms from me in a town loaded to the gills with worms for sale. To make matters more hopeless and unbearable, Dad was sitting in the same room waiting to see how I was going to pull it off. Situations like this were to be avoided at all costs. The stress level was off the chart. I was doomed before I started, and I knew it.

"Bob's bait shop," someone answered.

"Uh," I said, trying to avoid looking at Dad.

"Bob's bait shop, can I help you?" he repeated.

"Uh, ya," I struggled while staring at my shoes, "I w-w-was w-w-wondering if I had s-s-some w-w-worms that y-y-you c-c-could sell m-me?"

Well, that was my closer on the deal. Poor Bob was probably waiting to see if I asked him if he had Prince Albert in the can.

"What in the heck are you talking about? I don't understand one word you said," he shot back.

To throw more fuel into the humiliation fire, Dad took the phone away from my clenched hand.

My Dad interrupted. "Bob, Sam Andersen here. My son wanted to know if you have a need for any night crawlers at the moment. They have about twenty gallons of them. Oh, I see. Thought we'd call and check. Thanks, Bob."

Dad hung up, probably embarrassed by my miserable attempt at manhood in the high-flying business world of worms. My infamous sales pitch line became a family joke instantly. It took a long time before I could participate in the humor of it all; a long, long time.

On occasion, I'd go pheasant hunting with Mike and some friends. We'd spend a Saturday in February walking the cornfields and being startled out of our wits every time a bird would jump into the sky with the familiar loud squawk they make. It's a wonder we never shot one another. It could have easily happened. By the time we collected our composure to take aim, the birds were long gone. On the many hunts I attended, we never bagged one bird.

Once, after returning home from such a trip, Dad asked what we'd been hunting.

Now, I meant to say one simple word, "pheasants." But it came out "rabbits."

"Uh, ph-ph-ph-ph-rabbits," I blurted out.

Sheeesh! Not only did I fail to come up with a suitable replacement word for pheasant, but I also didn't even stay within the same species. Mike busted a gut laughing, and this episode as well became a family favorite over the years.

Since the pheasant population was left intact by our lack of hunting skills, we decided to now give the duck world a try.

Hunting ducks is different than hunting pheasants. The main difference to me was the need to get up so early in the morning to get ready for the high-flying birds to come in for a landing. At least this was the prevailing duck hunting rule with the older guys in our group.

I used to go hunting now and again with Mike and his friends who could drive. We'd arrive before sunup when it was cold and frosty, waiting anxiously for any warmth to brighten our mood. In those days, there must have been a shortage of ducks because we seldom saw any. If we did, they were always too high to shoot down, but that didn't stop us from trying. After a while, we just wanted to shoot the guns to hear the explosion, feel the kick on our shoulder, and smell the burned powder. We must have been close with our aim a couple of times because some of the ducks stopped laughing as they flew over.

Once Mike shot at a seagull, a rare sighting back then, and he actually hit it, but it didn't fall out of the sky like a dead duck, which drops like a sack 'o spuds. This bird kept circling and circling, driving Mike crazy with fear. When it finally did fall to earth, we were surprised to see how big it was. He imagined every game warden in the state was hiding behind all the trees around us waiting for him to do something illegal. He was almost paralyzed by the thought of becoming an instant felon, so he hid it under some brush and we got out of there. Mike told God if he made it out of this ordeal, he would never do it again. I think he kept that promise, but you'd have to ask him.

Having no luck at all with Mike's hunting friends, one cold day some older friends of mine took me out to a reed-filled slough. We'd been told this was a great place to hunt ducks, but we would have to wade out into the water and hide amid the cattails and water reeds. I borrowed Mike's chest waders, certainly looking the part of a duck hunter. Waders looked like bib overalls with attached boots all made out of rubber.

It was such a pleasant surprise to go duck hunting and actually see some ducks. The reeds were about five feet over my head as I slowly waded into them. I could hear my friends talking back and forth, but we couldn't see each other, even ten feet away. Ducks were flying everywhere, right over the tops of the reeds. I was blasting away and could see them fall. This was what real duck hunting was supposed to be like. Anxious to see my first kill, I hurried to where I thought it went down, forgetting the first rule of wearing chest waders: Never hurry when in deep, frigid waters while wearing chest waders.

My foot caught on a root, and my body's momentum took over from there. It wasn't a splash sort of fall, it was more of a choreographed slow-motion *Titanic* move. There was a giant sucking sound as the polar water rushed in over the top of the suit. It filled my boots first, then my leggings. The next part was particularly painful and took my frosty breath away. Then the icy water rose all the way up to the top of the waders. The extra weight brought my head down into the water, gun and all.

Regaining my balance, I made my way to the shore. I must have weighed four hundred pounds. I had to spread out on the boat ramp with my feet on the higher ground to drain the water out of my waders. The guys were all aware of what had happened to me, but weren't about to quit hunting with all the ducks flying around. It must have been hard to aim while convulsing with laughter. I took off the wet gear and my clothes and squeezed as much water out of them as possible, then sat in the back seat of the car shivering and waited for the trip home. Even though I finally brought down a waterfowl, I never got to see my dead duck.

I had a twenty-gauge shotgun that I had acquired from a student barber for ten bucks when I was twelve. What he hadn't told me about the gun was a major oversight on his part; the gun had a huge flaw. I learned about it one day when hunting, again for ducks, with Mike and his high school friends.

I was sitting on the ground waiting for the phantom ducks to show up with my gun pointing in the direction of the lake and into a dirt embankment which was about fifteen feet away. I didn't know, even after owning this gun for two years, that when the safety was on and the trigger was pulled, it was as though I had just cocked it to fire. By moving the safety lever to the off position, this would release the firing pin and the weapon would fire without pulling the trigger.

Dave Henry was walking along in front of the embankment when I flipped off the safety lever. Much to everyone's surprise, a blast from my gun, and a smoke-filled hole opened in the dirt pile just behind Dave's legs. Had it happened two seconds earlier, I would have blown his legs off.

After inspecting the smoking hole, Dave turned and looked at me with wide, questioning eyes. I did my best, despite my heightened state of anxiety, to tell him it went off by itself.

After re-creating the event, we all saw I had a bad shotgun. The older guys were sympathetic to me, and I appreciated it. I destroyed the gun by throwing it into the lake. No one would ever go hunting with me carrying that thing around anyway. Shame on the barber for selling me an accident waiting to happen. Of course, if I didn't find out about it for two years, maybe he didn't know about it either. That's the last firearm I would own for fifteen years.

Our school had two examples of similar mishaps by friends or family. Of course, it was devastating to both parties involved. One of the victims, Carl Hendricks, used to hang around the town pool hall most of the time. He had a small mouth which contributed to his crooked teeth. He combed his hair like a hoodlum, or "hood", as we referred to them, but he was always decent to me. I had not known him prior to the accident. Apparently several years before, his cousin accidently shot him on a hunting trip. His right leg was blown off above the knee. He was overweight and swore like a sailor, but surprisingly enough, was usually in a merry mood, at least while in the pool hall.

Being a couple of years older than me, I had a built-in respect for him and for his lot in life. He played a lot of snooker, a billiard game with a larger table, smaller balls, and rounded smaller pockets than an eight-ball table. It took extra skill to drop the balls with any regularity. He, however, could slam them in with amazing accuracy while his stump hung uselessly beside his good leg. He'd hop around the table cussing and laughing as he beat everyone he played. I was good, but not that good. I'm not aware what happens to fellows like that. People fade away from a kid's life like snow melts off an April lawn. I can only hope he led a happy, productive life, but I wouldn't bet on it.

This faulty gun episode did have a rather latent negative side, however. I thought how incredibly lucky I had been in not crippling Dave. Over time, and after several near misses in other events of my short time on the earth, I convinced myself that apparently the ultra-bad things that sometimes happen in life were never going to happen to me. After all, I had survived the 200-foot drop off the cliff in Sioux City when I was three. I hadn't choked to death on shards of glass at Grandma's house. I hadn't drowned when I fell through the ice witnessed by my cousins. I hadn't fallen off the water tower, and I had even avoided wearing the blue dress.

Somehow I never brought into this charmed life equation the fact that I struggled to say my own name half the time. Nonetheless, it would take some large doses of reality in the future to set me straight on whether or not I was a modern-day Achilles.

When I was eight, Dad told Mike and me that he would be bringing home BB guns for both of us. Holy smoke! Our lives were about to change. We were giddy for days, which turned into weeks. Every afternoon we waited for him on the front steps to get home from work, only to be disappointed that this wasn't the day. He had to know the wait was causing us great pains, but wait we continued to do.

Finally, he made good on his promise. Neither of us understood why he bought the guns in the first place. It wasn't Christmas or our birthdays, and we hadn't been particularly model sons, but we figured; why look a gift horse in the mouth? We had our BB guns! After the obligatory rules orientation concerning shooting each other's eye out, we went to do the bird population some damage.

We shot at anything that moved except kids, cars, cats, and dogs. After a while, as most things do, the initial excitement wore thin, but my aim improved immensely. Once I shot at a bird that had just flown into the top of a fifty-foot blue spruce. I didn't aim, just sort of a shot from the hip. Down it tumbled, branch after branch after branch until it hit the ground. To my dismay, it turned out to be a blue jay. We liked blue jays. They have a captivating birdcall and are beautifully colored. This was a bird of summer, unlike sparrows.

Mike and I made a pact that summer birds were off limits; robins, cardinals, goldfinches, and orioles. The plain birds, the blackbirds, starlings, sparrows, and doves were all still fair game. We also decided that red-winged blackbirds were just plain mean. Even though they had some red and gold color on their wings, it was still okay to blast them away. They'd dive bomb us when we were in the vicinity of their nesting areas, usually around reed-filled areas in ponds and ditches. With these critters, it was more about self-defense than anything else.

I enjoyed many lazy summer days toting my BB gun around the lakes and sloughs. Frogs were plentiful and even turtles. I'd drop dragonflies mating on cattails. I'd climb on top of boxcars at the railroad tracks and pick off sparrows for hours. I'd walk along the tracks for miles looking for something to shoot with my trusty BB gun.

---

Once, a friend and I were on the railroad tracks outside of town when we came upon what was left of the Martindale's home. We had heard it burned down a couple of weeks prior but hadn't bothered to see it yet. Everyone in town knew of the Martindale family. The father, Otto, was a short uneducated drunken man who worked odd jobs from time to time. Often I would see him loading boxes of fresh carp onto big trucks at my father's workplace, Stoller Fisheries. He was always unkempt, out of sorts, and usually three sheets to the wind. He also reeked of body odor. His oldest son, not only looked like him but was following his dad's example to a tee. Otto and his wife had thirteen children. Everyone in the school, no matter what age they were, had a Martindale in their class. My class had Annie.

The Martindales were on county welfare and lived on the proverbial wrong side of the tracks. I'd seen the house plenty of times in the past while walking the rails. Lots of kids and dogs were running around the structure that wasn't much more than an added-on shanty. It seemed like with each new kid, they had added on a little more house. I always wondered what it would be like to see the interior, but knew I never would or could. When walking past the Martindale's place on a Saturday, the wonderful smell of freshly baked bread filled the air. The mother would bake several dozen loaves, enough to last the family all week. I always marveled at the dicotomy of such a heavenly aroma escaping from such a hellish existence.

Annie Martindale wore hand-me-down dresses to school and looked like she seldom bathed. Everyone felt sorry for her but avoided getting close enough to carry on a conversation, at least not the boys. She must have been lonely.

Once in fourth grade, the class was discussing plant life and seed planting. Mrs. Westinberger asked us for any tips we might be aware of to ensure a successful germination of seeds.

Several plausible answers were made, then Annie raised her hand. We all looked her way. Annie never raised her hand. The Martindales were not known for spontaneity or any real thinking at all. There was a sense of dullness that pervaded the entire family. They could have easily been happy in the hills of the Appalachian Mountains.

"Annie," asked the teacher, "do you have anything you'd like to add?"

Proudly she offered, "Make sure you plant the seeds right side up, so the roots don't grow up in the air."

Today, I have the desire to find that little girl, hold her close, and tell her what a great answer she gave and everything will be alright someday. I want to assure her that sooner than she knows, she will be able to move and make a life of her own, making better decisions than her father did. That's what I want to do now. However, kid life isn't like that. Sadly, adult life isn't either.

Instead, we all broke out laughing. She tried to hide her head under her desktop. I'm so sorry, dear Annie. I know what you're feeling, but hiding your head in your desk isn't going to help. I've tried it many times.

———————

After the fire at their home, no one I knew could tell me where they went. I'm sure the county was glad to see them go.

We jumped over the temporary fence to inspect what was left. It was as close as I'd ever been to the place. We spotted two anxious dogs that could have been retriever mixes tied to a post. Their ribs were showing. They must have been left unattended for several days without food or water. Thankfully, at least, it had been raining, so water had been available in small puddles.

Nearby we spotted a 55-gallon drum about a third full of what was once dried dog food that had been soaked a time or two from the rain. When we looked inside, our stomachs turned. The meal was "alive"; the food was covered with maggots. The ravenous dogs were in a complete meltdown frenzy, attempting to get at it.

We didn't see any other choice; we tipped the barrel over, untied the ropes, and watched them both disappear into the barrel gobbling the maggot-meal. I'd never seen hunger displayed like that before. When leaving, we had to decide if we should tie them up, hoping the owners would be back, or let them fend for themselves. We chose the latter.

I'd carry my BB gun with me whenever I had random time on my hands. At this age, it was pretty much always. There was usually something worth shooting: signs, posts, trees, garbage cans, or trashed cars; anything that would make a sound if I hit it.

One day a bunch of us kids were sitting on the curb wasting valuable summer daylight. A boy, staying with his grandmother for a week, asked me a question, "Would you shoot me in the chest with your gun?"

I had owned my BB gun for three years. This was the first time anyone wanted me to plug them with it.

I was surprised and answered, "I can't do that. It would hurt, you'd tell your Grandma, then she would tell my dad."

"Oh, it won't hurt me. It's just a little BB gun. I promise I won't tell anyone," he insisted.

Apparently, he was trying to impress my sisters, who were also there.

"Okay, you promise you won't get me in trouble?"

"I swear," he swore.

I slowly lowered the barrel at his chest about five feet from me and squeezed off a round. His eyes widened and began to tear up. He ripped open his shirt buttons to find that the BB had broken his skin. A tiny bit of blood appeared, and the BB fell to the ground. He immediately ran home and told his grandmother what I had done.

In less than five minutes, a police officer pulled up beside us. His grandmother hadn't bothered to call my parents; she went straight to the cops. The policeman asked me why I had shot the boy.

"He w-w-wanted m-m-me t-to," I cried. He took my beloved gun away from me, never to be seen again.

Summer nights were endless. It wouldn't get dark until ten o'clock. We'd always have a bunch of neighborhood kids over to play hide-and-seek, hopscotch, or jump rope. For some reason, we didn't have a basketball hoop set up anywhere, which was too bad. This was the best time to learn a useful sporting skill. High schools don't offer varsity hide-and-seek, and I certainly couldn't become a letterman by being a great hopscotcher. Sometimes we just ran out of stuff to do.

On those nights, I'd walk down to the lake and fish all alone. There were plenty of empty docks to use.

I remember one silent night in September. The lake surface was like a black mirror. It was unusually quiet as I sat on the end of the dock with my legs swinging over the sides. I noticed the dark eastern horizon becoming lighter and lighter. In the next few minutes, I witnessed what was to be the largest, most orange harvest moon I would ever see. It was as if I had been transported to another planet.

I didn't understand moon cycles then, so I wasn't expecting a full moon, let alone one like this. It came up on the opposite side of the lake; I saw not only th0e one in the heavens but its perfect reflection as well. It filled the black sky and it filled the black lake. I was lucky to be there on that magical night and not off playing hopscotch. I've carried the memory of that magnificent harvest moon with me all my life. I've seen almost sixty of them since then, and none has compared.

Movies were always a great summertime diversion. We had a runt of a theater in town that charged twenty-five cents for a ticket, a dime for popcorn, and five cents for a Coke.

*The Creature from the Black Lagoon* kept me out of the lake for a while, especially where there was seaweed, and Steve McQueen's, *The Blob* was unnerving. I was hoping the Arctic stayed frozen. *Tarantula* was too scary to sit through; I paid my money and left before it started. Mike couldn't believe I'd do such a dumb thing.

We saw the 1958 version of *The Fly*, which was way too frightening for me. Our family saw it at a drive-in, so I was forced to watch it. Everything was fine until the woman tore the black cloth off her husband's head. Looking back at this shrieking lady was her beloved husband with a fly's head. The hairy black head came with huge green compound eyes and mouthparts that protruded out twelve inches.

I wasn't prepared for that moment with all the blood-curdling screams of the woman and the loud music. In fact, I had real nightmares for a couple of years afterward. Mike would wait until I crawled into bed some nights and then make a buzzing sound. I kicked and screamed to make him stop. Once I kicked him in a place that put his buzzing sound into a higher octave.

In 1956, when I was seven, I went to see *The Ten Commandments* starring Charlton Heston, Yule Brynner, and Anne Baxter. For some reason, I went alone. This was the perfect kid movie. It had everything jammed into three hours; color, excitement, good guys, bad guys, beautiful costumes and ladies, war, palaces, chariots, disasters, and revenge.

Today I find it a little strange that Moses was forty when he left Egypt and eighty when he returned to confront Pharaoh, and that neither Pharaoh nor his Queen had aged a day. Even Hollywood should have to answer for that stretch of the imagination.

That being said, I was enjoying the movie very much, then something unexpected happened to me. When Moses came down the mountain from the burning bush encounter and met Joshua, his countenance had changed.

This affected me in a way I can't describe. I had been touched beyond my understanding. The experience was totally unsolicited and unexpected. I wanted to "know" who he had been talking to on that mountain. At that moment in time, I had such longing, such desire to know much more about what was a predominantly confusing subject.

There came into my young heart a euphoric feeling of wondrous love and understanding that was telling me everything would turn out alright. I wish I could say I've had several more of these episodes since, but I can't.

I walked home that night alone and decided to do a strange thing. I knelt under the giant old elms in our yard and gave a child's prayer to a God I knew so little about.

Being only seven years old I could only utter, "Dear God, please let me know you better so I can feel that feeling again. Amen."

What I was actually asking Him, with my limited knowledge and capacity, was to someday let me understand Him in a more complete and less confusing way. That he might lead me along a path so that someday I might come to a greater knowledge of where I came from, why I was here, and where I was going.

Sixteen years later, in my last month of college, He answered that little boy's prayer.

**The neighborhood gang.**
**Circa 1956**

**Mike and me.**
**Circa 1951**

**Proud of that new bike.**
**Circa 1955**

# CHAPTER TWELVE

# BACK TO THE FARM

One thing about being stuck on a farm in the summer as a kid is that, once there, I was really stuck on a farm. If I were to run out of things to do on hot days, nothing could save me.

A couple of times the folks sent me to spend a week with Uncle Jack and Aunt Jeanette on their farm outside of Spencer. Their sons, Mark and Brad, were a couple of years younger than I so it could have been worse, but it was taking me away from my beloved Okoboji in prime time.

Jack farmed a 160-acre spread, and like most every other farmer in Iowa, he grew corn, soybeans, and alfalfa. Depending on the month, he could be doing any number of chores around the yard or out in the fields on his tractor: plowing, disc harrowing, or planting in the spring; spraying weeds or cutting and baling alfalfa in the summer, or harvesting crops in the fall. These are just some of a farmer's work detail in the field.

When he wasn't in the field, he might be tending to his cows and pigs, or mending fences or repairing the gamut of machinery it takes to keep a farm on a paying basis. Sometimes Mark and Brad would be attending some scheduled lesson or appointment which would leave me alone with nothing to do. My aunt would send me out with a cold bottle of water to find Jack on his tractor. I'd walk over the fields and spot him moving slowly down the rows. He was always ready for a long cold drink of water by the time I got there. I'm sure my aunt appreciated my help. Walking in corn fields wasn't easy, and apparently ice chests hadn't been invented yet.

One of the most captivating happenings on the farm was when my aunt decided to kill a chicken for dinner. Since they roamed the barnyard unmolested, she would spread a little chicken feed so the hens would gather around her. This made it much easier to catch one.

Once that was accomplished, she'd pick up one end of a solid steel bar that weighed at least ninety pounds and laid it on the chicken's neck, pinning it to the ground. Every time I saw her do this, I watched with great interest. Placing her foot on the bar, she then grabbed the doomed bird by the legs, and with one quick yank, separated the chicken's body from its head. The spectacle was fascinating to watch, but what came next was downright bizarre.

She'd let go of its legs and off went the headless chicken, running around the yard squirting blood like a volcano and bumping into everything. I'd often heard Dad use the expression, "running around like a chicken with its head cut off", and now I saw it for myself. Good heavens, what a strange horror to watch. As grizzly as it was, I couldn't take my eyes off it. No kid could have. The show must have lasted two or three minutes before the hen ran out of blood and fell down. The question still remains; was she actually dead while doing all that running or not until she toppled over?

Let me tell you a variation of this tale: Years later I read a story of Mike, the headless chicken. The owner had missed the main artery in the neck and a small part of the brain while chopping off its head with an ax and the blood clotted before it could bleed to death. The ghoul began traveling with the freakish hen to shows around the country. He fed it with a syringe. Old Mike lived for two years and finally choked to death in a Phoenix motel in 1947. My aunt's chickens didn't have such luck.

I helped do chores with the boys when it was time. Every farm kid had chores. Manly farm-kid chores like slopping the hogs, milking the cows, stacking hay bales, and putting up silage. My city-boy chores consisted of taking out the garbage, sweeping my half of the garage, shaking the rugs, and vacuuming the stairs. Just a different mindset, I suppose. No wonder I once wore a dress to impress a girl.

Sometimes there might be a dead chicken in the coop. It was always astonishing to see the pigs fight over its carcass after we'd throw it into their pen. Pigs eat anything. The sound of them crunching those bones taught me to never fall down in their presence. When Dorothy of *The Wizard of Oz* fell off the fence into the pig pen, I was alarmed for her. I knew what they could do.

Although Jack eventually added plumbing to the farm house, we still used the outhouse when we were outside, which was pretty much all day. It was a two-holer, and none of the guys thought it the least bit strange when someone our own age joined us while we were in there doing our business. I can't think of one good reason to have a two-holer today. What are the odds that nature might call two of us at the same time? For guys on the farm (and everywhere else), the world is their urinal, so the outhouse was used for one purpose only.

Again, Iowa is hot in summer. There are several kinds of hot, however, and one of those is "outhouse hot." There's no more miserable place to be than sitting in an outhouse in Iowa in the summer. The only thing that could make it any more uncomfortable would be for my uncle to join me on the next hole over. Seriously, what could we talk about?

"Gee, Uncle Jack, last night's chicken tasted mighty good. You just missed the coming out party?"

He did tell me a story, though, and for him, it was pretty funny.

He started out, "A couple of guys were sitting pretty much like we are on a two-holer, when one of them stood, pulled up his pants. A quarter fell out of his pocket and into the hole. The man reached into his wallet, pulled out a five dollar bill, and tossed it in there as well.

The other man sitting there watching all this unfold asked him why he just threw a five-spot in the hole. The man standing told him that he was not going to climb in there for a measly quarter." Like I said, for Jack, that was pretty funny.

Outhouse humor had to be brought in; no one would spend a second longer in there than was required to read a bathroom joke book.

Once I was sitting on one of those holes, wondering if bumble bees ever flew down inside, and if they did, wouldn't I be giving them quite an obvious target? I dismissed the thought as soon as it ran its course through my head. There was no point in frightening myself on such ridiculous fantasies. I would have heard about something like that happening.

To my utter amazement, not a minute went by before I heard the familiar buzzing. I looked over at the hole beside me and watched a fuzzy yellow and black bumble bee fly out of it. I was amazed at what I just witnessed. What could the odds possibly be? I jumped through the rickety old door with my pants around my ankles and fell to the ground. I could never bring myself to use the outhouse again. I tried once, but couldn't relax enough to even start the job, let alone finish it.

Speaking of horrible out houses: The Spencer Fair had a twenty-five-holer. I had asked someone where the bathroom was, and they directed me to an old long wooden building that hadn't been painted since the thirties. Inside on the left was a long metal trough on the floor used for the urinal. On the right were at least twenty-five wooden holes in a row without seats or privacy walls. Above the holes were several openings in the wall where windows had once been.

I can't even describe the overall condition of the place. I tried to hold my breath as long as I could, but to no avail. The stench was inescapable. Seated on one of the holes was a skinny old man with soiled long underwear around his lower legs. He looked right at me and smiled a toothless grin. Everything about this place was too horrible to imagine spending any time there.

I have vivid memories of lots of my past experiences and mostly this blessing has its advantages, however, the multi-toilet memory is one I wouldn't mind forgetting. Unfortunately, after fifty-five years, I doubt it's going anywhere.

Going back to the farm: Once my brother Mike spent part of a week with me at the farm, and he brought along his dog, Tiny. He was actually the family dog, but Mike loved him the most and was his chief caretaker. We were out with Uncle Jack riding on each side of the tractor on the fenders while Jack was disc harrowing a field. Discs are similar to two-foot diameter pizza-cutter blades attached in rows to several axles, which are pulled behind a tractor. Jack's disc may have had up to thirty of these circular blades which are used to chop up weeds and last year's crop.

Mike and I were passing the time riding high on the John Deere with Jack and checking on Tiny while he ran along beside us. He was a small dog, low to the ground, probably a Pekingese/Terrier mix. He should never have been allowed to be anywhere near this machine. Tiny was much too small to keep up, even with a slow tractor and he was exhausted.

He managed to stumble on a large dirt clod and fell beneath the disc blades, practically cutting him in half. Mike jumped off the tractor after Jack stopped and ran back to the writhing, snapping dog in the throes of death. Mike was crying and reached out to hold him.

Jack yelled, "Don't touch him, Mike, he'll bite your hand off!"

My sobbing big brother heeded his words and watched Tiny die. I was crying, too, by now. Not so much due to the dog's death, but for Mike.

We got a shovel from the tool shed and buried him under the row of poplar trees. Mike was distraught at first but got over the tragedy in a few weeks.

The next year during the Fourth of July get together and after the dead pig episode, all the cousins decided to dig him up and see what he looked like after all this time. We found his bones and made jokes about it. Mike says he wasn't around for the sick-o party. He may not have been.

One evening at another family gathering at the farm, Jack's third son, Ricky, came running into the house screaming about his "teece-teece", which was the family's potty-training word for penis. He was around four years old and quickly became a favorite among us older cousins simply because he was so darn cute. He and some of the older kids had been out playing with the only horse I ever saw at the farm. It was a Shetland type for kids to ride. I never did. Horses instinctively knew I was nervous around them and always did what they could to keep that relationship going.

Rick was crying, and the other kids were explaining to his parents that the horse must have bitten his privates.

"Horsey bit my teece-teece, Daddy, horsey bit my teece-teece," he repeated over and over. They examined him right there in the kitchen. Actually, there wasn't too much to see. After all, he was only four.

Of course, all of the older boys were grabbing themselves purely in a defensive move and imagining how much something like that would hurt. Even in our state of horror, the element of humor found a way to float to the surface, as it always does when you're a kid. However, if we knew what was best for us, no snickering was allowed until we got outside. Once out there it spilled over into the usual back slapping and howling until we could control ourselves again. We then could return to the house and express our concern and sorrow.

Uncle Jack, however, found no humor in what had just happened. He got his rifle, went out alone to the corral, and shot the horse dead where he stood.

Apparently everything turned out fine for Rick, who is a father today.

In the early mornings, I'd accompany Jack to the barn and watch him milk seven or eight cows. He had some sort of milking machine with four sucking devices that attached to the cows' teats. With two sets of these milkers, it took over an hour to complete the process.

After collecting the milk, he separated the cream in his electric separator. He poured the warm milk into a large stainless steel hopper or bowl on top of the machine and turned it on. I noticed it also had a hand crank attachment on the side. After all, it hadn't been too many years since the rural areas of America had been electrified. There were two spouts in the front, one where the cream exited and one for the skimmed milk. He poured the cream into a clean, expensive looking stainless steel container with a tight lid. Jeanette took it from there. I guess she sold it to a dairy store.

Jack hauled the leftover milk to the pig trough and mixed it with field corn. The hogs ate it in less than a minute, pushing and shoving all the while trying to get more than their share. It seemed like a lot of trouble to go through to feed some hogs.

During the actual milking time, which was about twenty minutes per cow, Jack stood in front of an open window of the old barn. He'd brush away the latest cobwebs and stare out at the horizon in deep thought, smoking his Camel straights. He was dressed in his greasy blue pants, shirt, and a John Deere cap. He didn't seem particularly happy being a farmer.

Not too many years later, he figured out that selling farms paid a lot more than working them. He got his real estate license, and soon Mom and Dad were talking about how he had just closed his first farm sale, making ten thousand dollars for himself in commissions. About the same my father earned in a year at that time. My mom was thrilled for Jeanette. I imagine my dad was a little jealous.

They moved off the rented farm, bought a home in town, and Jack joined the Spencer Country Club. He later learned to fly an airplane and even bought a Cessna 150 to take his clients to view properties.

Once he flew me down to college in Ames after a break from school. Seeing Iowa from the air is like looking at a huge green checker board. We never had a lot to say to each other, unfortunately. Being cooped in a Cessna cockpit for ninety minutes certainly accentuated that.

Jack had come a long way from sweating in the fields, waiting for someone to bring him a cold drink of water on a hot day.

One summer I spent half a week at the farm and the other half in town, about fifteen minutes away in Spencer, at Uncle Carlo and Aunt Norma's home. They had two boys, Greg, two years older than I, and Kirk, one year younger. These are the cousins I think of when the subject of hysterical laughter comes to mind. Greg certainly had his serious side, but he loved to laugh, probably more than any of us. One day I gave him something to really laugh about.

The three of us walked out to visit Pete's Pond outside of town. The pond was actually a holding tank for the city's sewage treatment facility. All the toilets in Spencer were connected and ended up there. Somehow all the solids were removed from the sewage waste water and stored in this large holding area. I never knew who Pete was, but he must have been someone held in high regard.

The surface of the pond was like none other I'd ever seen. Surprisingly, the smell wasn't overpowering, as long as it was left undisturbed. Of course, just looking over a scum covered pit was not enough of an adventure. Kids always have to test the waters, even though this stuff was not water or even close to it.

The crust was about four inches thick. When I walked out onto it, the surface had an undulating motion quality; a smooth, predictable wave. It could be compared with jumping on a dead beached whale and almost as smelly. It was a puzzling sensation. I had no fear because no one who lived a charmed life like mine could ever fall into something as horrifying as a pond o' poop.

The next thing I knew, the crust cracked I slipped through the surface and into the pond o' poop.

Instinctively, my arms stretched out, stopping my descent at chest-level. I was helpless as well as terrified that this just might turn out to be an ugly situation or, shall I say, a worse situation than it already was. This muck had a lot of the same qualities as quicksand, and it was slowly sucking me down.

Horror and utter delight are two expressions that are supposed to be on opposite ends of the scale; a true dichotomy. Greg and Kirk somehow managed to overcome this dilemma with shrieks of alarm then yelps of laughter. They eventually grabbed my relatively clean hands and pulled me out.

Gadzooks! I was covered in a black tar-like goop that no amount of shaking, stamping, or jumping could remove. I didn't want to scrape it off with my hands in case I needed to scratch my nose. Arms lifted, I waddled back to their home. Did I mention the smell? I shouldn't have to.

I'd heard these boys laugh before in all kinds of different situations, but never like this. When we got home, they hosed me off in the back yard, naked. We didn't bother to save the clothes. We deposited them into the neighbor's garbage can. Carlo split a gut when he got home from work and heard the story. He was my favorite uncle.

Later on that week, Carlo came home for lunch after working the morning hours in the men's clothing store where he was a salesman. He complained to me about something poking him through his pants near his backside and asked me to help him out and look for it. He said it had been bothering him all morning.

I took a look as best I could, but found nothing. He wondered if he had sat on a staple left on a chair, or maybe a small thorn was lodged in his seersucker suit pants. Aunt Norma was in the kitchen just shaking her head.

I looked and looked in the vicinity where he thought it was. This went on for quite a while.

"I think I know where it is for sure," he said, pointing to the center of his butt. "Let's hurry and get this done. I'm late for work."

I looked exactly where he told me. "C-c-carlo, I j-j-just don't see anything s-s-sticking out."

"Well then, you've got to look real close to make sure," he instructed me.

My nose was almost touching his pants when he let her rip. A big blast of methane released right in my shocked face. It took me a second to realize that it had all been a ruse. Norma was now convulsing in the kitchen. I instinctively slapped him right where I'd been searching.

"Oh, Carlo," I blurted out, "how c-c-could you?"

Like I said, he was my favorite uncle.

**Jack Holiday in his farming days.**
**Circa mid-1950's**

# CHAPTER THIRTEEN

# STUPID IS AS STUPID DOES

Spirit Lake's first high school was built in 1916 according to the concrete plaques over the two east entrances. I remember thinking how old the building was when I first noticed them. This would have been 1956, or forty years after its completion. I figured everyone alive in 1916 was dead. I also associated that year with movies where all the people were filmed in black and white and moved in short jerky spurts without a soundtrack. They were always depressing to watch for some reason; maybe it was the lack of color. I put Disney's *Steamboat Willy* in that same category because every time I watched Willy, a bit of melancholy overcame me. I hated that stupid whistling mouse; everyone did. Except Mr. Disney, it made him a zillionaire.

That building eventually became the junior high when our new high school was built in 1961, or 54 years ago, at the time of this writing. To me, it's still the new high school. Some kid today looks at that 1961 plaque and probably wonders the same thing I did about the 1916 plaque. Heck, we hadn't even walked on the moon yet in 1961.

It's funny how kid-time is so different from adult-time. Waiting for birthdays or Christmas to come around for a kid is torturous, like clock watching. For adults, the rent or mortgage payment day comes around at warp speed. Life can be compared to a spinning roll of toilet paper; the nearer to the end you get, the faster it goes.

In the old high school, the gymnasium was built in the middle of the building in the basement with wooden bleachers surrounding it on all sides on the floor. There were also bleachers on the next floor up, the first floor, and when looking down at a basketball game from that vantage point, there was a gladiator arena atmosphere associated with it. Absent air conditioning, it also had the same smell.

The bleachers folded up close to the walls when not in use, and we elementary kids walked by them every day for lunch or music class. One day I thought I would tempt fate and run my right ring-finger fingernail, with my palm facing me, along the wooden slats. I wanted to see if I could get all the way to the end of the hall without jamming a splinter in it. It seemed like a lofty goal at the time.

I was keeping up with the rest of the class at normal walking speed when in less than five seconds a jolt of pain exploded up my arm. Reluctantly, I looked at my finger to see what damage I'd just done. Beneath my fingernail, all the way down to the cuticle was a sliver of wood that, to me, looked like a two-by-four. The teacher escorted me to the nurse, who winced and called my mother, advising her to take me to the doctor.

The good doctor said he needed to dig under the wooden beam to pull it out, so a local painkiller injection would be required first.

Not totally sure what injection meant, I asked, "D-d-do y-y-you m-m-mean a sh-sh-shot with a n-n-needle?"

"Yes, but it's a small one," was his lying reply.

Doctors and dentists, especially dentists, always call their needles small ones. These are the same small ones they pull out of the bottom drawer in the next room and hide behind their leg before you open your mouth.

All this occurs just before they say, "You're going to feel a little pressure."

Needle-hiding and different ways of saying, "This is going to hurt like hell," must be some of the first courses they teach in medical and dental schools.

Doctors and pain were synonymous in my mind, so I insisted I didn't need the dreaded shot for him to get the small tree out from under my nail, as I thought the shot would be in my butt like it always had been. To me, there was not much difference between a shot in the butt and sitting too long on Uncle Jack's two-holer and being nailed by that bumble bee. I was quite adamant about not having the shot.

Instead of a tiny pinprick to numb my aching finger before he started digging around, I went with the other option. This other option was to experience all the pain while the doctor slammed his pliers under my already throbbing and bleeding nail to eventually find a good place to grab onto and pull the splinter out. This was proving to be my second big mistake of the day.

Mother of pearl! Removing that timber hurt worse than when I got into this mess. I imagine some of the patients in the waiting room got up and left after hearing my yelps. The profuse bleeding started, and the doctor applied some ointment to the wound, which sent me through the roof. Apparently, ointments had to hurt to work. Anyone still in the waiting room must have headed straight for the exit.

He wrapped my finger with gauze and tape. It was finally over. I held my smoldering hand with guarded relief.

Here's the irony of it all:

"Lee," he said to Mom, "he's going to need a tetanus shot, just to be safe."

Yep, right in the butt.

The Marion Hotel was one of the oldest buildings in town which housed mostly single older folks who rented long-term. I delivered newspapers there when I had my paper routes. It was always handy to have these customers because I could rid myself of over ten papers in short order on snowy days within the warmth of the old building. It was also the stop I made before going to Smokey's across the street to order my two rolls and a Pepsi.

Collecting from the customers who lived there was always a little depressing. These were old, forgotten, lonely men and women, mostly men, who came here to live out the rest of their lives. They had tiny rooms and a bath down the hall. The smell was an ancient odor of stale coffee, cigarette smoke, and unmade beds. The lighting illuminating the narrow hallways was poor. Kids usually viewed geriatric strangers with a bit of melancholy. It reminded them of what may be in store later in life, even if it was seventy years down the road.

Knocking on the doors on collection day was usually done in great haste, wanting to get out of there as soon as possible. I didn't know how to speak to such old, presumably sad people. Lots of these guys were World War One veterans. One man had half of a left foot having a shoe made just for his handicap. Every one of these people had a story to tell. Stories of home, youth, love found and love lost, and of family. They harbored stories of successes in business and eventual failures. As they added nothing but years to their resumes, they gave up more than they ever thought they would, finally succumbing to the inevitable; living life on a monthly stipend, an acceptable form of surrender.

Spirit Lake had a lot of old veterans for being such a small town. Every Memorial Day we had a parade with the WWI vets in one bunch, the WWII vets in another, and the Korean War vets bringing up the rear. My dad marched with the WWII group, by far the largest one. Almost every man in town over thirty and under forty-five identified with that group. To belong to that age group and not be a veteran must have been tough to live down, even though we still had to have men on the farms back home during the war to feed the nation and the troops. Living in Iowa, there were lots of men around who fit into this category.

To kids, all these wars seemed so long ago, even the Korean War, which may have been only four years prior. The Korean War wasn't mentioned much as I grew up. It was a mystery war that had spawned helicopters and not much else, except human history's longest staring contest at sixty-three years and counting on either side of the thirty-eighth parallel.

The older WWI vets hung around the small downtown area as I was growing up. They were missing limbs and using canes, and I saw this as a sadness to be avoided if possible. Living life with a leg or arm missing seemed incomprehensible. During the parade, I didn't feel a sense of pride like I do now, but a sense of foreboding, almost like watching *Steamboat Willie*.

This feeling of hopelessness was also apparent when a caravan of green Army trucks full of soldiers would periodically move through our town in route from one fort to another. I watched the young men drive by, smoking and waving. I would wave back, but this dark mood was overpowering whenever they rolled on by.

I knew it was peace time, but it seemed that every twenty years or so a major war was fought, and I did the math. If WWII ended in 1945, then 1965 would be my turn, my war. Would we have one to fight then? I was hoping there wouldn't be.

Of course, I didn't know it at the time, but President Eisenhower was already sending advisors into Southeast Asia hoping we could nip communism in the bud before it blossomed.

----

I brought up the Marion Hotel for a reason: A couple of years before my fingernail incident, I spotted what turned out to be a striped gopher on the sidewalk adjacent to the hotel. On the north side of the building was a dirt lot used primarily for parking.

When I first saw the gopher, I didn't know what it was, but it was cute and I wanted it for my own. Until then, I'd never had any luck catching anything of real value. Turtles, fish, salamanders, frogs, toads, baby birds, or butterflies didn't count because anyone can acquire those, and they weren't something you could pet. I wanted a pet-able pet.

I started running after it like I had done before with a mouse, a squirrel, and once, even a baby raccoon. In the past, without fail, I would lose them in the brush or some hole. It turned out this fuzzy guy had nowhere to hide.

The gopher ran alongside the building frantically looking for somewhere to ditch me. I was surprised the chase was lasting as long as it was. It had never happened like this before. The gopher and I circled the entire building one time, and I was gaining on him. After all, it was summer, and he wasn't designed for long-distance running. The Marion tenants were sitting in metal chairs on the front veranda. This was the pastime of choice on hot summer days, and they were looking on with unusual interest.

When the gopher got to the parking lot side of the hotel the second time around, he spotted an empty soup can lying on the ground and scurried into it, probably thinking it was a hole. I ran to it and victoriously picked it up. Anxious to see his cute furry little face, I held the can in my left hand, grabbed him by the back of the neck with my right hand, and pulled him out. His teeth disappeared.

In slow motion, I saw his two long yellow front teeth sink into the back of my right thumb. I still have the scar.

Surprised and horrified, I dropped him where I stood and ran home crying. I don't remember the pain associated with the bite as much as the betrayal. Why didn't he like me? I liked him.

Mom called Dad, who suggested she call her friend Irene who lived down the block. Irene had cats, so maybe she might know something about critters and rabies.

Rabies?

I bit more about Irene: I knew she had cats, two Siamese house cats, because every week I was paid a quarter to do odd jobs around her place. One of those jobs was scraping enough sand for her cats' indoor sandbox from underneath her back porch. This was a pile of sand probably left there from its construction many moons ago. As the months went by, it became more difficult to gather enough to fill the box. I hated that job. There were cobwebs under the porch, and the sand had already been used by every cat on the block for years. The only difference between the sand under her house and the smelly sand in the sandbox that I was replacing was … actually, there was no difference.

In the winter, I had to shovel an opening to squeeze through the snow. The frozen sand then had to be chopped out in chunks and smashed down so it could be used. Most of my childhood I assumed a sack of sand was unaffordable since she was making me work like this. Eventually, I found out sand was basically free. I wanted to ask her about this, but she had moved.

The cats would watch me do this job all winter, and somehow that made me feel inferior to them as if I was working for them. The old adages, "If your sweet kitty were large enough, it would eat you" and "To a dog, you're his master; to a cat, you're staff," applied to these cats. I had it in for the two Siamese cats in Disney's *The Lady and the Tramp*. They deserved everything they got.

———————

Back to the critter: Irene sat me down with her encyclopedia, and we started looking through pictures to determine what exactly had bitten me. Due to my speech pattern, we had it nailed down from a rodent of some kind, to a small zebra.

Eventually, we went back to the scene and asked one of the old tenants who witnessed the chase from the front porch of the hotel. He told her it was just a striped gopher and that he sure enjoyed the show. Since the rodent hadn't attacked me, and that I was the perpetrator, they decided not to begin the painful twenty-six shot rabies treatment. I was probably going to be okay. Of course, busy-body Irene suggested that I get a tetanus shot.

Yep, right in the butt.

A couple of years later, I was walking to school after a delicious breakfast of french toast. I was in a good mood, looking forward to the day. I had just crossed the street in front of our house and spotted a bird sitting on an electrical wire. I picked up a rock and threw it at him. It sailed over the bird and over our neighbor's garage. The funny thing is, the moment I let the rock go, I wished I could've taken it back. I grabbed my head in fearful anticipation knowing this could end badly. If I could've just had these premonitions before I acted, it would have saved me a ton of trouble as a kid.

I heard a loud sickening crash, then I heard a man yell. It was Butch Busby, the Chief of Police. He lived there. He put his head around the corner, gun drawn and saw me standing there like a sap.

"Doug," he asked, "was that you?"

"Y-y-ya, Butch, it was m-me," I admitted. My rock had landed on the windshield of his police car.

"Holy crap, boy," he exclaimed. "I thought someone was shooting at me." That's when I noticed he had actually drawn his gun out of his shiny black holster.

"I was just coming out the door when I heard, what I thought was a gunshot. What the hell would make you do something like that, Doug?" he asked

"I-I-I d-d-don't know, j-j-just stupid I g-g-guess. Sorry, B-B-Butch," I stammered.

"Well, you better get to school. I'll call your dad and let him know," he said.

I was about to have one of those long days at school, but still not wanting it to end because I would have to go home and face Dad. I was grounded for a week; not for being bad, but for being just plain stupid. Dad made that crystal clear, it was becoming my trademark.

As stated before, summer nights can be endless. Regular games of Hide-and-Seek, Red Rover, or Captain May I became routine. We'd need to invent other forms of activities. There were many bats ever-present in the evening sky. Their main diet was mosquitoes, which were always in plentiful supply. Every kid knows what Barney Fife knew; "if a bat gets in your hair, you go crazy." We all knew they had hooks on their wings used to grab a tight hold onto our scalp. Nonetheless, we still wanted to catch one and keep it for a pet.

I borrowed a dish towel from Mom and wrapped a large stone in it, tying it tight with twine. The idea was to throw the weighted towel into the air as high I could, and a bat would collide with it, getting his hooks tangled in the process and it would bring him down. It sounded so plausible to all the neighborhood urchins. We were always on the lookout for any low-flying bats that might get stuck in our hair, though. None of us wanted to go crazy. We should have been more concerned about low-flying stones wrapped in dish towels.

To get maximum height, I'd rotate the sling-like device around like a propeller, not unlike David did with his slingshot against Goliath. When I figured I had just the right speed, I'd let it go. There I was surrounded by six to eight kids in the dark, throwing a toweled stone into the black sky. What could go wrong?

After a few attempts, the inevitable happened. The two-pound missile came crashing down on Janice Simmonds' back making a thud-like sound. It knocked the wind out of her for a moment, so she didn't immediately start crying or screaming, which, in itself, is quite alarming. Eventually, she regained her breath and let it rip. She went running into her house explaining to her parents how I hit her with a big stupid rock, omitting the part about her consenting to our master plan to bring down the winged mammals. The bats were pretty much safe on our block after that, not that they were ever in any danger in the first place.

Once on the way to Omaha from Okoboji, our family drove through Council Bluffs, Iowa, on the eastern side of the Missouri River. It's named Council Bluffs for a reason. My siblings and I had never seen anything higher than rolling farmland until now, and we were having fun pointing at the next big mountain as we called them.

With all the excitement in the car, we were making a big impression on the folks as to our potential enjoyment of visiting real mountains. This may have given them the idea of our first ever summer vacation. That and my little sister, Debbie, was now six and could handle it.

Whatever the reason, our first family vacation came when I was ten. One day in June Dad announced that we were going to the Black Hills of South Dakota. We were thrilled beyond measure, having no idea what the Black Hills were.

Thankfully, our parents didn't tell us a month before or we would've driven them nutty. It was a week out, and both Mike and I had to get friends to take over our paper routes, and I had to bring my lawn mowing up to date. Once that was done, we were good to go.

We left on a Friday evening late so Dad could drive all night for us to roll into a small park in Deadwood, South Dakota by mid-morning. When we arrived 500 miles later, we unpacked some picnic stuff and ate Underwood's Deviled Ham from little cans wrapped in white paper, on Wonder Bread. What a great start for our vacation. Dad had fallen asleep on Mom's lap in the shade.

We were looking at real mountains now. The air was clear, the sky blue, the sun bright, and I had my first smell of a pine forest. This was a smell that I could never forget.

A small detail I forgot to mention. Before we left our house, Mom had told me to go to the bathroom, which was located upstairs over the kitchen. Knowing I would be sleeping and dreaming in the back seat of the car, it was a good move on her part.

Since I was the last person to use the bathroom, I figured a little science project might be in order. I wanted to know how much water would be collected in the sink if I plugged the drain with the rubber plug-on-a-chain. I allowed a little drop of water to drip out of the faucet while we were gone for the week. I estimated it would be about half-full when we returned. Since our sink didn't have an overflow drain, this would be a perfect experiment. Of course, I wanted to keep the project to myself, and I did.

The first day we visited attractions that everyone comes to the Black Hills to see. One of them was an old gold mine. All of the mining or cave attractions were mostly kid-proof, not nearly as much fun as it would have been had we found one on our own and explored it. However, Mike did find a chunk of pyrite (fool's gold) on one side of the asphalt path. He couldn't believe his magical run of luck and was excited beyond measure.

It's nearly impossible to convince a kid who finds a chunk of this junk in a gold mine that it's not the real thing. The park rangers probably dropped the stuff around to add a little excitement for the kids on an otherwise boring tour. He wouldn't part with that pyrite for years. He kept it in his top drawer. I'd show it to my friends from time to time, never letting on its real name. Why spoil the fun?

We stayed the rest of the week at Spearfish Canyon Lodge, in the most western part of the Black Hills. It was night time when we showed up there, and on the way, Dad spotted some boxes that had apparently fallen off a truck. He stopped by the side of the road and told Mike and me to help him gather up the bowling pins lying all over the place.

This was a side of Dad I didn't know. He had gone to all the trouble of stopping the car on the side of the road with a sleeping family to glean bowling pins. The Dad I knew would've driven past someone else gathering bowling pins in the dark, calling him the stupidest sucker he'd ever seen. This time, he was the one that found them first so that description didn't apply here.

We began loading all we could see into the trunk, at least twenty of them. Bowling pins were bigger than I ever thought them to be. They were fifteen inches high and weighed three or four pounds each. We already had a fairly full trunk, so we had to stuff some of them onto the back seat floor. What was Dad thinking he was going to do with them? We didn't have a fireplace to burn them, and we certainly didn't own a bowling alley. I guess anything free was hard for him to pass up. We also found a box of folded socks. Mom was especially pleased with the socks.

We pulled in front of our cabin at the top of the entrance driveway. It was a pitch black night, and the smell of the cool pines was overpowering. We unloaded our bags and the kids ran around the inside of the cabin. It smelled of old treated wood. The floors were varnished pine slats that creaked with every step. The walls were split pine heavily coated with shiny yellow varnish as well. The ceiling was vaulted and open to the rafters exposing a few cobwebs hanging from one to the other. Even the furniture was made out of pine. The kids were to sleep on the floor in the back room. It was perfect.

After exploring all three rooms, opening every drawer and closet, Mike and I went outside to see what we could find in the dark. We ran around the front of the cabin, then down the roadway a little. We saw several other cabins placed along the road, but ours was the best. Finally, Dad called us into bed. We would have to wait until morning to explore every inch of this awesome find.

Soon, after daylight appeared, Mike and I awoke. Our parents were still sleeping since they hadn't had a full night's rest from the time we left Okoboji. Mike and I jumped out of bed and looked out the screen window. We were shocked to see what we were looking at; the tops of the trees! This back room was no more than a screened in porch cantilevered over the edge of a cliff.

We ran outside to take a closer look. To our amazement, we were at the very edge of a 150-foot drop-off. There was no fence, no railings, and no night warning lights to let anyone know not to venture out there in the dark. We could have most assuredly fallen to our deaths the night before. I guess my charmed life motto had kicked in again and spilled over onto my brother as well.

After taking it all in, we began throwing rocks over the edge. We'd never thrown a rock that far in our lives, and it was intoxicating. After a short while, stones weren't entertaining enough. What else could we launch over the side? We could hear the rocks hit the bottom, but we couldn't see them. What could we find that would be easy to throw and easy to spot all the way down to the floor of the ravine?

"I know," I exclaimed, "B-b-bowling p-p-pins!"

Once in a blue moon, Mike would agree with me. This was one of those times. Without a second thought on what Dad might have wanted to do with the pins, we unloaded them out of the car, all twenty.

What a hoot! They were perfect throwing objects. They'd spin all the way down and then crash into the trees below. Who needs a bowling ball when you have a 150-foot cliff?

When Dad discovered what we had done, I felt safety in numbers. After all, wasn't it my big brother's job to keep me from doing stupid things? Dad expressed his dismay in losing his pins, but not much else was said about it. Maybe he didn't want to start off the second day of our wonderful vacation on a sour note. I know Mom was probably pleased we didn't have to haul the ridiculous things home, and she still had her box of socks.

Dad went all out making sure we saw everything the Black Hills had to offer. Mount Rushmore was awe-inspiring. I remembered hearing about it in school from time to time. The monumental sculpture had been completed only eighteen years prior to our visit, which, to a kid, was sometime between Moses and Columbus.

We even got to eat lunch in the Rushmore Dining Room adjacent to the huge window that framed the four Presidents' heads. This was a rare treat, usually reserved for the lucky stiffs in my way of thinking. I remember seeing the Hitchcock movie, *North by Northwest* with Cary Grant and James Mason many years later. I was thrilled to see the room, where I had eaten a buffalo burger, play such a prominent part in the movie. It looked just as I remembered it. Iowans seldom get to see landmarks they visited so close to home used in movie locations. *Costner's Field of Dreams* and *Dances with Wolves* would be the only other ones that come to mind.

We visited Wind Cave, rode the ski lift at Terry Peak, and got to sleep through a Passion play one night. We stopped at Wall Drug and the Badlands on the way back. We even went to Devil's Tower in Wyoming. As a result of this side trip to Wyoming, I knew what Richard Dreyfuss was sculpting out of mashed potatoes on his dinner plate, then later in his basement before most of the audience did in the movie, *Close Encounters of the Third Kind.*

One of the most exciting adventures of this trip happened when Mike and I decided to climb a huge hill one morning. After all, it was there to be climbed, and we had time and energy to kill. When finally at the top, we looked down and marveled at how far it was to the road below. From there we had two options; walk back down, or roll large boulders down the hill to the roadway at the bottom to see how many trees they might take out in the process. It was a tough call.

We began rolling boulders, unaware of the unbelievable speed these granite missiles were capable of gaining. What the catastrophic damage one of the boulders could cause was immense. They'd start out slow, then pick up speed quite quickly. They ran over any small trees in their path, jumping and hurdling toward the bottom. What exhilarating fun it was. We hadn't one thought of where these boulders might be landing at the end of their journey. One could have easily taken out a car on that road, spoiling a perfectly good day for the occupants. The boulders could have gone through the walls of the cottages that lined the road. We just kept rolling; we had never had an opportunity to do anything like this before, and may never again.

I heard a faint voice. Mike launched another one down. We both heard the muffled voice again and decided to quiet down to listen. We heard something far away, but couldn't make out what was being said. Scanning the bottom of the hill where we thought the sound was coming from, way down on the road, we could see Dad. He was as little as an ant and yelling something at us.

Assuming he probably wanted us to come down, that it was time to go, we started back. He wasn't particularly upset with us upon our arrival, but he pointed out the stupidity of what we were doing. Only then did it dawn on us how lucky we had been that none of the boulders had caused anyone any harm. Again, my charmed life had kicked in to save the day. I was convinced.

Our car's bumper had been stickered every time we took in a sight on the trip. We had maybe fifteen in all. When we got home, Dad told me to wash the car. In the process, I scrubbed off all the stickers that adorned both the front and rear bumpers. He asked me why I would do a thing like that without asking him.

Apparently, these were a badge of honor to display for a couple of weeks. Dad wanted people to know he dragged around four little kids for seven days and that he was a devoted father. I would have to agree, it was quite an accomplishment.

I explained, "I th-th-thought y-y-you w-w-wanted a cl-cl-clean car. Sorry."

I thought I had done such a good job. Those bumper stickers were a pain to get off. I had to use Brillo Pads to do it. When Dad saw the scratches on his chrome bumpers from the steel wool, I heard about that, too.

Later on that day, I heard Dad and his friend Bill talking in the kitchen. It seems Bill had come to the house to check on things the day after we left.

Bill said, "Ya, Sam, I walked around down here in the kitchen to check the stove, the fridge, and the sink, and I heard something upstairs in the bathroom above me. That's when I found the plug stuck in the sink drain with a dripping faucet. I could hardly believe it. The sink was full and was just beginning to spill over onto the floor."

He continued, "So I pulled the plug, turned the faucet off, and wiped up the water with a towel."

"Man alive, Bill, you saved me from having a disaster when we got home. I wonder how in the hell that could've happened?" Dad asked. "Wouldn't that frost ya?"

I was turning white with fear. I could hear my heart beat. I had completely forgotten about my insane little science experiment. What an unbelievably boneheaded stunt. How was I ever going to explain this? I had nowhere to hide. I was trapped like a rat. I was the last one in the bathroom, and Mom knew it. Why, why, why do I keep doing these dumb things? It had taken only hours for the drops of water to fill the sink, not a week like I had figured.

"Gee," Bill added, "believe you me, Sam; you would've had the kitchen ceiling on the floor when you got back. Talk about expensive!"

This was serious. Running away was rapidly becoming a viable option. When was Dad going to line us all up and read the riot act until someone spilled the beans?

Sometimes things just turn out differently than expected. There's no reason for it; it just happens from time to time. I never heard anything else about the drip in the sink, leaving me to believe that Dad assumed it was just an innocent oversight. After all, in his line of thinking, no one would be so stupid as to do something like that on purpose.

*Au contraire*, Dad, *au contraire*.

# CHAPTER FOURTEEN

# MOVIN' ON UP

Dad came home one day with the biggest news of my life until then, aside from the hypnotist therapy. Dad had bought a boat! Living in Okoboji without a boat was like living in Phoenix without an air conditioning unit. It's not mandatory, but it can be miserable without one. I convinced myself that I was miserable without a boat because everyone else was having so much fun on theirs and I wasn't.

Eventually, most of us Lakers get a boat and our time was now. We were officially squeezing our nose under the tent of the Lucky Stiffs Club.

Dad bought a 1948 Chris Craft made of mahogany, with a 60 hp four-cylinder engine located in the aft section. He paid $500 for it. It was an inboard, which meant the propeller was attached to a straight shaft exiting out the bottom of the boat behind the engine compartment. The exhaust pipe protruded out the transom and made a Harley-Davidson sound when running under a concrete bridge at no-wake speed, which was mandatory under bridges. The familiar sound of, "potato, potato, potato," was unmistakable. That sound and the smell of the exhaust on the surface of the water always elicits remarkable memories of my childhood on the waters of Okoboji.

I was eleven and Mike was soon to be fourteen. The entire family drove down to Lazy Lagoon on West Okoboji Lake to take the first gander at our newest edition to happiness. The old adage, "The two best days in a man's life are the day he buys a boat and the day he sells the damn thing," doesn't apply in Okoboji, because you just buy a bigger boat. The Chris Craft was beautiful. The shiny, varnished, reddish-brown wood adorning the hull was so smooth and clean and breathtaking. I noticed the white grout lines separating the slats on the fore and aft decks and the bright polished chrome trim and cleats that were attached to the wood with oval-headed stainless steel screws. All of it was a sight to behold.

The small windshield and gauges, the floor-mounted forward/neutral/reverse gear stick, and the huge steering wheel adorned the interior. The red Naugahyde that covered the front and back bench seats, red/green running lights on the bow, and the flag pole mounted on the aft was all there in one glorious package. I figured my life was about to change in a big way, but I had to bide my time until I could take this baby out on my own.

We all piled in, Dad at the wheel, Mom, and Debbie beside him. Mike, Marcia, and I climbed in the backseat. Dad started the engine and slowly backed out of the slip. Once clear of the small old dock, he shifted it into forward, made our way out of the little man-made harbor, and onto West Okoboji. We had finally arrived.

Mike was allowed to take out the boat alone on the Fourth of July. Dad wasn't in town that week but called to tell Mom he was giving his permission. What a surprise! We forgot all about firecrackers and dead pigs. We had places to go without adults holding us back and watching our every move. We were growing up, finally.

This was the start of many fun-filled days of learning to slalom ski with our friends tagging along and helping pay for gas. I figured, however, if I didn't get to drive, I shouldn't have to help pay for any gas. I brought my case before Dad and rightfully lost it. One more person weighs down the boat and affects the performance, especially while being pulled out of the water on skis.

We all got pretty good at skiing. We learned to slalom by dropping a ski while on two, then picking it up later. We had crappy skis, no more than eight-inch wide pieces of plywood with half-inch wooden rudders attached underneath, so losing one would be no great loss.

Nonetheless, I got so confident that while slaloming I slipped the single-handled ski rope over my head and around my neck and yelled, "L-l-look, Mom, n-n-no hands!" Of course, Mom wasn't there. Mike stopped the boat and said I'd lost my turn. He was a good brother. I would've broken my neck had I fallen.

I can remember only two instances that Dad went out in the boat with his sons to spend some quality time. The first time we were miles away from our boat docking area when we lost the propeller due to a sheared cotter pin. This pin keeps the nut and washer in place which, in turn, prevents the propeller from spinning off the shaft. We had to be towed all the way back. I didn't get to show Dad my skiing skills that day. For some reason, I thought he would enjoy being dazzled by my water-sport prowess. The next and last time Dad was with us proved to be much more eventful. Water can be dangerous.

We were late getting out on the lake as it was early evening on East Okoboji. This time of the day normally had the best skiing conditions; no wind and fewer boats. It was warm and quiet. The sun was shining on us from the western sky just before setting, and I was still anxious to finally show Dad my skiing skills.

We were about to get started when Dad pointed to the eastern sky. A gigantic anvil-topped cumulonimbus cloud reaching 60,000 feet into the atmosphere was coming our way. The sun was colorizing this monster a reddish hue, but it was turning blacker by the second. The air began to chill, and whitecaps were forming on the surface of the water. We had to get off the lake fast.

As I stated before, the Midwest is famous for its thunderstorms. They can sneak up, hit hard, and leave everyone wondering why in the heck people live there. This storm was ugly and promising to be mean. Out on the lake is the worst place to be when a tempest like this one comes to town. There are many stories of lost boats and boaters in these lakes.

Thankfully, we were only a few miles from our dock and hoist located at Hafer's Boat Works. Glenn Hafer ran a relatively large marina in the area. He sold fuel, repaired engines, hulls, and even manufactured his own brand of boat, the Hafer Craft, painstakingly constructed out of slats of mahogany wood. This day he would be frantically trying to save every craft harbored in his place.

When we pulled into our hoist lift, we were glad to have one to use. Many boats were only tied to the docks and rocking on the water, which by now was fast becoming choppy. By the time ours was secured out of the water on the hoist, all hell was breaking loose around us. The winds were now bringing with them torrents of rain. Thunder was nonstop, and lightning was everywhere. In no time, the winds were 60 mph and causing the surface of the lake to heave to and fro.

Boats were becoming battering rams aimed at the docks and each other. Some were lifting up and toppling down onto the dock, punching holes in the hulls, then taking on water as they slid back, sinking to the bottom.

Some of the larger boats were also launching on top of the smaller ones moored beside them, causing them to scuttle. Several crafts had snapped their lines or lost the cleats that the lines were attached to which secured them to the docks. These boats were banging around like bumper cars, crashing into other crafts with their new-found freedom.

Some of the vessels were even hung up on the dock posts that had impaled their hulls like bullheads on a stringer. Several of us were out on the docks trying in vain to tighten down the mooring lines. It was impossible to fight these waves, and dangerous.

A canvas cover flew off a boat and slammed into Mike, blowing him off the dock and into the water with the tarp still draped over him. He kept his head and swam down and away from it before he surfaced. No one but him knew it had happened. It occurred so quickly and without warning. He could have drowned there easily. Most drowning victims die because they panic. He didn't.

We tried in vain to change the eventual outcome. The docks themselves were losing the battle and became unstable. Glenn called us all indoors to ride it out before someone got hurt, or worse.

As quickly as the storm began, it was over. Though still raining heavily, the freakish winds were gone and the thunder was more distant. Being too dark to see anything because the electricity had failed soon after we arrived, we ventured back out onto the docks with flashlights to look at the carnage. What a mess. Boats far more expensive than ours were sitting at the bottom of the lake, some costing thousands of dollars. It was hard to take it all in. I knew some of these boats and their owners. It would take thousands more to bring them back to life. We looked over at our $500 Chris Craft, sitting high and safe on our hoist and we were thankful.

The summer of my thirteenth year, Dad let me take out the boat alone. I had no idea what possessed him to come to that decision. I must have proved to him I was capable of following the rules of water safety, or most of them, and I was actually careful when docking. At slow speeds, most inboards lose steering response and preparing for this is crucial when pulling into a dock. I had displayed this skill several times over the last couple of years. Or maybe he allowed me this privilege because he let Mike do it at thirteen, and he only wanted to be fair. For whatever reason, I was loving it.

This was to be the summer of my coming out. I was no longer tied to my bicycle or out hitching rides. I spent every minute I could driving the boat with my friends. I mowed lawns just to buy gas for the privilege. I was a captain on top of the world and free to go anywhere I wanted around the entire Okoboji area. This was just a notch under driving a car.

East Okoboji is about nine miles long and West Okoboji is about seven. They join together under a bridge on the main highway that leads to Spirit Lake from the south. This spot was sort of ground zero during the summer in Okoboji. About a mile south of the bridge was Iowa's Mecca of fun, Arnolds Park, purposely spelled without the apostrophe. Living in Iowa created a love for Arnolds Park, and it seemed everyone made a visit there at least once a summer. I could now go there anytime I wanted by boat. This was a big deal for a new teen kid.

---

Arnolds Park is an amusement park built in the 1880's and located on the south shore of one of the bays of West Okoboji Lake. All the structures were made of wood and had neither heating nor cooling. The wooden roller coaster, The Legend, built there in 1930, still runs.

When I was a young boy, it was all about the park, but as a teen, it was more about the people.

Usually, three times a summer, out of the blue, our parents would announce that we were going to Arnolds Park. These were magic words to us. We never knew when it would happen. They wisely wouldn't tell us days in advance, because there would be no living with four crazies until we got there. We all would be absolutely giddy about the news. We spent the day finding all our neighborhood friends and telling them we couldn't play tonight because we were going to Arnolds Park and they weren't.

When we arrived, Mom would take my sisters, Marcia and Debbie, and visit the Kiddyland portion of the park, but mostly they sat on a bench, ate Nutty Bars, and watched the people. It was Dad's job to drag Mike and me around to all the big kid rides. I was curious why Mom didn't want to have any real fun even though she'd always say she did. Dad did his best to stretch his dollar, yet show us a great time. It was easy to spend ten dollars in the course of the night on the whole family.

We'd usually start out on the newest ride to come to the park, the Scrambler, situated at the north end. This newer ride was constructed out of aluminum instead of the old chipped painted steel that the other rides were made. The lights were not quite as bright there since it was the last attraction next to the parking lot. Mike and I had to learn to sit in the correct position on the seat to avoid being crushed by Dad's g-forces. We'd always want to ride again, but Dad was used to ignoring those requests. When walking, we'd pass by a popular bar located smack-dab in the center of all the action. Drunken men would stagger out of there. I always felt sorry for them and was a little frightened at the same time. I was glad Dad was with us.

The park had the Majestic roller rink for those who were compelled to skate in circles. I didn't know how to skate yet and couldn't understand why people would waste their park time in there. Where was the excitement? The organ music was depressing. It seemed to attract the older crowd, those in their twenties and thirties.

A walk around would bring us to the Bullitt, a long pole with a rocket-like cage attached to each end. Not only would the pole turn like a windmill, but each compartment turned as well. This was way out of my league. Dad and Mike didn't even want to try that thing. The operator would leave riders hanging upside down at the top until someone starting swearing at him or upchucking a perfectly good corn dog.

The park had its own resident Gypsy family that operated most of the rides and manned the fortune teller booths. I never talked to them, but felt like I knew them over the decades of my park attendance.

The main ride, The Legend roller coaster, was ever-present throughout the park because it was positioned in such a way making it impossible to avoid. The coaster weaved its way through most of the other attractions. It was noisy by itself, and with a load of screaming people, it was unnerving to me. I thought it was for bigger kids; I was only six. Dad would ask me from time to time if I wanted to go on it, but I reluctantly declined until one night, Mike, who had ridden it before, convinced me it would be so much fun.

Dad, Mike, and I walked up the stairs to the loading area. I was petrified and had to be encouraged to make the necessary steps to the top. We waited for the linked cars to arrive. When they did, they came in loud and fast, stopping abruptly and with great fanfare. The big people were exiting the opposite side, laughing and yelling. This was too much for me to handle. I told Dad I wanted to go back down and watch them do it. He stood behind me and assured me I would be okay. Remembering the sledding incident at Grandma's, I didn't dare disappoint him. He was in such a good mood.

Somehow Dad and I ended up in the front car, and Mike was seated with some stranger in the next one back. Mike was patting me on the shoulder, continually talking up a good story of how much fun this was going to be. When it was loaded, gravity took us down the track a bit to hook onto the big grease-ladened chain that would pull us up to the top. I knew I was going to have to see this through; there was nothing I could do about it.

There was a sudden jolt when we attached to the chain, and I yelled, "I w-w-want to g-g-get off, D-d-d-dad."

The coaster started its way up to the top with a steady click, click, click of the chain sprockets. About halfway to the top I was feeling better. This ride was actually kind of fun and not as scary as I thought it was going to be. The colored lights dotted the rest of the park. I could see it differently up here. We passed by oak trees and soon were even above some of them. I relaxed my iron grip on the bar holding me in.

I turned to Dad, "Th-th-this isn't so b-b-bad. I'm n-n-not s-s-scared at all!" He just looked at me and smiled.

We were finally approaching the top where there was a large sign overhead.

"W-w-what d-d-does that s-s-say, Dad?" I asked.

"The point of no return," he answered.

"W-w-what d-does that m-m-mean?" I asked.

He smiled. "Well, Son, you're about to find out. Hang on to the bar."

If this scene were to be played out in a movie, Dad would have been wearing red stretchy pants with horns protruding out of his forehead.

Sitting in the front car of the coaster, I got the first view of the drop-off. I don't know why I was surprised; I'd seen it a hundred times from the ground. What was I thinking was going to happen? Gee, maybe the operator knew I was just a little kid and he would somehow back it down the track as slowly as we climbed it? Well, he didn't, and the bottom dropped out of my safety zone world. My stomach must have moved into my throat. I hadn't been holding on to the bar tight enough, and I lifted out of my chair at least a foot. I slid past the bar that was supposed to be holding me in. Dad grabbed me and sat me down again. This was all happening with g-forces slamming me around. If I could have jumped out, I would have.

When it was over, I didn't say anything for a bit. Mike was laughing and wanting to go again. I was in the mood to find Mom. I would pass on the nutty ice cream bar.

Some Saturdays we spent the whole day at the park. Since we never had enough disposable cash to spend on rides all day, we went to the Fun House. For twenty-five cents, we got to spend as much time there as we liked. Even walking in the place was fun.

There was a series of shifting planks that made it impossible to keep a normal gait, plus a bunch of holes in the floor that blasted compressed air up to us. Any girl who was stupid enough to wear a dress or a skirt deserved what she got. There were coins glued to the floor, and people would bend down to pick them up, getting a shot of air in the face. The ladies in dresses would get a blast in the backside as well. I wondered if the man who controlled the air had to pay the Fun House to work there.

Once in, we had lots of choices. The mammoth four-lane wooden slide was always worth the time. We'd grab a small rug and run up the stairs to the top, place the rug on one of the lanes, hop on, and push off. There was one big drop then a smaller one. It was lots of fun and worth the walk up to the top.

Friction burns were common occurrences. This was a dangerous ride while wearing tennis shoes. If they slipped off the small rug, the rubber shoes would suddenly bring the slider to a halt, then tumbling down the slide head-first would result. It was always best to take our shoes off first. I can't imagine why that was not mandatory.

The Sugar Bowl was shaped like a twenty-foot wide Jell-O mold ring made of varnished wooden slats. While it was turning around, the object was to be king-of-the- hill on the center cap and keep everyone else down in the trough. I got pretty good at it, especially as I got bigger.

Even so, there were days when some big fat kid was king for the day on that thing, and no one wanted to challenge him. Eventually, some hoodlum-looking guy with his smokes wrapped in his t-shirt sleeve would crawl up there and throw fat-boy on his butt. We'd all cheer, but then who was going to challenge the new tough guy? Sometimes we were content to just lie back on the far side of the revolving bowl and watch the world go round. It was always hot and sweaty in the Fun House, the swirling air was a godsend.

The Barrel was a cylinder laid on its side which continually turned around. It was six to seven feet in diameter and thirty feet long and also made of varnished wooden slats. The object was to attempt to walk through it without falling down. Many of us took off our shoes and sat on its floor as it rolled up behind us. We'd see how far up we could stick before sliding back to the bottom. We spent hours doing this. It took little effort and was quite relaxing. Sometimes we came down on someone trying to walk to the other side, causing them to fall on us. This was frowned upon.

I used to see older guys stretch their arms to the top of it and hold their position while they turned with the barrel, similar to the famous Da Vinci drawing. Later on, I could do it too, but knowing when to make the first real attempt was the trick. I tried several times when I thought I was tall enough, only to find myself upside-down with little support and then crumbling on my head.

After several hours running around in this place in the summer, we all needed a bath. The place smelled like a high school gym during a wrestling match. At the top of the slide was a long screened opening that faced the lake. We'd sit up there and enjoy the refreshing air while it dried us off. Looking out the window, we'd see people out on the lake swimming, skiing and sailing in the bright, lazy sunshine.

In the evening, Arnolds Park was lit up with colored lights. The aroma of caramel corn, hot dogs, cigar smoke and even boat exhaust fumes on the water, gave this place all the ambiance a kid could ever want. We'd even wear our swimsuits under our clothes so we could jump into the lake near the big lollypop-shaped pier adjacent to the park. This all-day fun could be had for only a quarter.

In my mid-teens, Arnolds Park turned into a people meeting place. The park had one well-traveled road that ran between all the buildings and the lake. We'd drag this road for hours several times a week. Everyone's car had just been washed, and anyone with a convertible was envied until winter set in.

My first time as a cruiser was with Dean Holbrook, who owned a 1958 Chevy Bel Air. His parents owned a small store on Big Spirit Lake with a gas pump on the dock where he worked during the day. He always had plenty of money to buy me hot dogs, drinks, drive-in tickets, and popcorn. This was unusual, but I let him do it.

He and I dragged that park on a regular basis my fourteenth year for one summer. We'd pass the same oncoming traffic twenty times before changing directions to see who else was there. The first few passes were full of laughs, hearty waves, and the usual crude one-digit salutations.

After a while, it turned into the lifting of the chin to acknowledge their presence for the tenth time. Even later on a pinky finger raise would do or an eyebrow movement. Near the end of the evening, we were looking at our shoes rather than making eye contact. That's when it was time to grab a snow cone and head for home. The underlying reason for doing any of this was to somehow meet girls. We never did. This sophomoric mating ritual still remained the primary magnet to the park.

The Roof Garden was a big deal in Okoboji. It was a second-floor dance hall built on top of almost everything at Arnolds Park except the rides and the Fun House. The massive window shutters would fold down to allow the lake air to circulate through the place. Tuesday nights were reserved for the big draws in entertainment. People drove to the park from all over the state to be there. Names like Roy Orbison, Bobby Vinton, The Guess Who, the Everly Brothers, the Turtles, Jerry Lee Lewis, and the Beach Boys were just some of the shows. In my parents' day, it was Glenn Miller, Artie Shaw, Stan Kenton, and Benny Goodman.

The stage was only one foot higher than the dance floor and no security ropes to keep us at bay. We could literally stand three feet away from Brian Wilson singing "Surfer Girl" and "Don't Worry Baby."

My biggest regret was not doing exactly that. I was either dancing or looking for someone to dance with. What a shame. I did, however, get to see Orbison up close sing "Crying." I was so close; in fact, I could see his uvula shaking away in the back of his throat and caught a glimpse of his eyes hidden behind the oversized dark glasses. Absolutely everyone in Iowa, no matter what age, has memories of the Roof Garden and Arnolds Park.

The Roof Garden usually booked a headliner band on the Fourth of July. Folks from all over Iowa, South Dakota, Nebraska, and Minnesota would come pouring into the place. We'd take the boat over to the park to avoid the traffic jam and tie it up on any free dock space we could find. Later on, when darkness fell, a fireworks show was given. There were hundreds of boats, all with their green, red, and white lights dotting the black lake, making for a glorious sight to behold. After every explosion, there would be continuous honking of the boat horns to show their appreciation.

The ride home from the park by boat was always an anticipated experience. The roar of the engine and the swish of the dividing waters as we slipped through the surface was soothing. The glow of the bow and stern lights, and the navigating of the buoys located near the shallow areas of the lake were part of the whole trip as well. Spotting our dock on the blackened shoreline, hoisting the craft, and even the walk home; all were memorable ingredients of life in Okoboji in the summer. I was living large.

Sometimes I would take the boat out alone just to be on the lake when it was calm. I'd sit on top of the seat and drive, feeling the warm air on my face and the sun on my back. On my way home from one of these sessions, I thought I'd see how close I could come to a buoy at full speed without hitting it. Full speed in this boat was about 35 mph. I misjudged my position and hit the metal buoy on the starboard side. It punched out one of the mahogany slats on the side of the hull. I was lucky, so lucky, that it was above the waterline, or the boat would've sunk then and there.

I took it into Hafer's to have the hole fixed. This meant no boat for anyone for a week or more. Summer was only twelve weeks long, so this was unfortunate. I told Dad about it, but not the part about me being stupid again. I didn't need to mention being stupid anymore; it was pretty much a given by now. When he was particularly upset with me, he'd tell me "everything I touched turned to crap." Disagreeing with him on this assessment was pointless; more than not, he was right.

After a week, I went down to Hafer's with my twenty-five dollars, all the lawn mowing money I had, ready to hear the damages. He showed me the final result of the repaired hull. The new wood piece matched perfectly. He charged me seven dollars and fifty cents. What a guy.

When I first started taking the boat out, Dad had already built his own small dock with a lake access permission slip he got from someone. Mike and I helped him put it in. It was only two planks wide, but it worked for our purposes. He bought a hoist for fifty bucks and had me paint it with bright silver Rustoleum paint. Our unpainted dock looked particularly sad sitting beside the brilliant silver hoist, so I decided to paint it. It would be a surprise for Dad when he came out the next time.

I bought what I thought was an oil-based product. It was white, it was liquid and could be spread with a brush, and it was cheap. It said white wash right on the can. I thought of when Tom Sawyer painted, or rather, had all the neighborhood kids paint his aunt's fence. He had used a whitewash, too. If it was good enough for Aunt Polly's fence, it was good enough for our dock. What I didn't know, and apparently neither did the salesman at the hardware store, was that whitewash is really just liquid chalk.

It took me half a day to finish it. Of course, I started at the closest point, the shore, and worked my way out to the end of the dock. Instead of painting myself into a corner, I painted myself into the lake. I had to swim to the shore.

That evening I told Dad about it, so we went down to see how the job turned out. The dock looked great. It was already dry, which surprised me because paint usually took a day or more to thoroughly dry. We walked out onto the planks, and that's when he asked me what I had used. When I told him whitewash, he shook his head and said we were going to have a big mess on our hands for some time. He couldn't yell at me because of my good intentions, but I could see his frustration in dealing with this dilemma.

Our shoe prints needed to be washed off with a wet towel every time we got into the boat for the next month. It only stopped because most of the whitewash on the dock came off when it rained. No wonder Tom Sawyer was tired of whitewashing his aunt's fence.

**A Chris Craft runabout, similar to Dad's 1948 model he bought for $500 in 1960. Today, this boat (restored) is priced at $40,000.**

**The Roof Garden was ShowTime magic, with the Fun House next to it.**

**The Legend, the oldest wooden roller coaster west of the Mississippi River.**

**Funhouse Museum in Milford, Iowa.
The Slide, Sugar Bowl, and Barrel displayed.**

**The Funhouse interior with Sugar Bowl and Barrel Roll pictured.**
**Circa 1960**

# CHAPTER FIFTEEN

# LEARNING TO LIVE WITH IT

Junior high seemed to be the time when school suddenly got serious. No teacher was looking out for me anymore; nobody holding my hand throughout the year. The various classes were divided among several instructors, and the grading was based on performance.

Either the student cared enough to do the work and receive a good grade or he didn't. The assignments were left more up to the individual to master more than ever before. It was also becoming apparent who was stepping up to the challenge and who wasn't. The kids were becoming divided into higher and lower groups, and even though friendships transcended these boundaries, there was still a pecking order of distinction that had reared its ugly head. Everyone knew who belonged where.

I was in the top thirty percent though I believe most kids probably had me pegged lower. I was slow to raise my hand to answer questions posed by my teachers because it just wasn't worth the trouble or possible embarrassment. When asked directly to give a response to a question, I might start out with some offering. Realizing then what words were coming up that I knew I couldn't say, I would fain ignorance and end up offering my surrender words: I don't know. I learned to say that phrase without hesitation because I used it a lot.

It was similar to being in a jail cell and gazing out through the bars at the world, wondering if I would ever be a real player in it.

Handicapped people do learn to survive. They develop certain skills that bring them a measure of success. This provides a little shot of endorphins to their system, a small ray of light into their life. The realization of these discoveries encourages them to develop these helps further, to hone them.

My ray of light was developing my sense of humor along with one of the trickier aspects of humor: timing. I discovered that I could come up with funny comments about almost anything. These were quick, sharp, and to the point. If an explanation was ever needed, it was a total failure and an embarrassing one at that. I learned to avoid these disasters as I went along.

To my surprise, I found I could do this without my handicapped speech pattern coming into play, and it gave me a boost of confidence. I could now contribute to the current conversation, in my own way, without the need of crawling into a hole.

This was all fascinating as it developed, but while in class, I was getting dirty looks from my teachers. My constant interrupting with some clever outburst that resulted in classroom laughter was not endearing me to them. I became the proverbial class clown.

Mr. Ron Bemise was my English literature teacher and a dedicated one. He was younger than most of the others on the staff and had a lot of energy. He was a naturally entertaining man, which is a plus when teaching David Copperfield to adolescents. I was behaving in my new normal way in his class and, for some reason, I thought he liked me in spite of it. Maybe he did, but he would have liked me more if I was in someone else's English class. Even so, he would more often than not crack a smile whenever I offered up one of my comedic gems.

When I got my first quarter report card, he gave me a D+.

On the back of the card he wrote, "Doug is a very disturbing element in my classroom."

Ouch! I was hoping my parents wouldn't be turning the card over to find that glaring accusation, but of course, they did, and I got both barrels when I presented it to them.

My relationship with Mr. Bemise changed after that, totally on my part, I'm sure. I was leerier now and thought of him as sort of a traitor, an untrustworthy teacher, especially since I never saw it coming. I was more withdrawn in English class than before, and it may have been my awkward way of giving him the cold shoulder. I have no doubt he loved my new tactics, as it was allowing his job to be so much easier. I had also gained a new respect for him, something every teacher needs from their students.

Some of our other instructors tried other, more direct ways of gaining respect. Mrs. Woodsen would slap a face at the drop of a hat. She was just slap-happy. Even though she had to be in her sixties, I'd seen her do it several times. She was a grey-haired, skinny woman who wore lots of rouge and way too much perfume, which actually would blow her cover some of the time. We could smell her coming down the hall at forty paces.

I finally got mine when she caught me running in the hallway after school. Back then I had a perpetual cold and must have missed the tell-tale odor. I was never in one of her classes, which leads me to believe she was lying low, waiting for me to someday make a wrong move so she could finally get that Andersen kid. After all, in two years I would be moving on to high school, and she would've missed her chance.

I guess while classes were in session during the day there may have been a disciplinary line a teacher couldn't cross without being labeled an outright abuser. An unwritten rule that suggested I won't slap your students and you don't pummel mine.

Adhering to this rule, she never bothered me during school hours. After school, however, I guess everyone is pretty much fair game. Mrs. Woodsen asked me why I was running in the hall. Before I could utter a word, she slapped me across my face. She said something else that my ringing ears missed, and without provocation, slapped me on the other side of my face. She did this probably in case she'd never have the opportunity again.

Another teacher, a tall, portly man, monitored the students in lunch lines and assemblies. Whenever he didn't like what someone was doing, he'd whack him on top of his head with a wooden yardstick. I say "him" because girls were either off-limits or better behaved. The kicker was; he had glued a thumb tack near the end of it. I imagine it drew blood, but I never had the pleasure of being a recipient. He must have been abiding by the unwritten corporal punishment rule of no whacking my student since he was never my teacher.

I'm betting whenever he struck, he turned the stick over so the tack side was turned up; that it was only a scare tactic for all to see. Wherever the truth lies, it worked. We'd glance down at the end of it as he walked by to see if the glistening point was still there. It always was.

The junior high study hall was on the third floor of the old high school and was the largest single room in the building. There were at least a hundred kids in there biding their time waiting for lunch. It was supposed to be a quiet hour reserved for study and was monitored by various instructors; this particular time by Mr. Chaparral. He was a math and science teacher in his fifties and a no-nonsense kind of man.

Once Marla Cox raised her hand and complained, "Mr. Chaparral, these boys are bothering me by playing pool."

The desks we sat on were from 1916 and still had the inkwell holes drilled into the upper right corner. In our day they were used as a great catchall to avoid being caught with pea shooters, marbles, gum, playing cards, and the like. A quick swipe and all the evidence ended up down the hole in an instant without having to open the lid. Dan and Roger had discovered a new use for the holes: pocket billiards. They were using pencils for cue sticks and spit wads for balls.

The monitor's desk was located on a two-foot high stage in the front of the huge room.

Mr. Chaparral screamed, "They're playing pool?"

He was off that stage and halfway across the room in no more than three strides. I'd never seen a teacher move so fast or deadly. When he got there, he hit Danny's head so hard it actually bounced off his makeshift pool table twice. Roger had time to block his blow, so he got two of them instead. I was sitting right across the aisle from all this horror and was shocked to witness such unbridled rage directed at these boys. It wasn't as though they had been doing some dastardly deed that would have warranted such a harsh penalty. Maybe he was in a nasty mood because he'd forgotten his lunch box at home and would be forced to eat lettuce sandwiches with the rest of us.

It wasn't over either. They were both sent to the vice principal's office where they each got three whacks with the Board of Education.

Everyone knew about that swat board the vice principal, Mr. Farber, had hanging on a wall in his office, which was located adjacent to the study hall. Fifth grade through eighth grade were somehow designated "swat-able" years. If we were sent to the vice principal's office for any rule infraction during that span of time, we might very well end up having to hold our ankles and get what's coming to us. Even though I was sent there for a variety of reasons, mostly class disruption with my wisecracks, I only had the pleasure of the paddle used on me once.

All the study hall students would be quietly working away when suddenly and without warning loud cracking sounds would fill the air, usually three in rapid succession. We'd all be waiting to see who got it this time. Mr. Farber's door would open and then close. It was now time for the perp-walk.

Some kid would walk into the room with a smirk on his red face, doing his best to convince us his butt wasn't on fire. I always admired them for that and wondered if I would be so brave. Once we heard ten whacks in a row. Not only did we all want to know who it was, but what he did to deserve ten swats.

When Charles entered the room, he was wearing a sheepish grin and wanted us to believe he didn't feel a thing, but his tears betrayed him. That and the fact he couldn't sit down at his desk for the rest of the period.

My turn came when I was sent in there one too many times. Mr. Farber asked me to turn around and grab my ankles. I'd heard from other recipients that he made you pull down your pants as well, which was always the great fear I had. I was relieved when this turned out not to be the case and that all those years of dreading this day turned out to be nothing of any consequence. I looked forward to walking through the study hall with a smirk and my manhood intact. Delinquency may have its merits.

Back in English class, Mr. Bemise announced that we were to divide into five groups of six students. The groups were to each select an American author to study. Then every student in the group was to read a book written by that author. A month later the groups were to be brought before the class, and the members would give a detailed book report. It would be a big part of our grade.

I sat there listening to the teacher's explanation with my ears burning. I walked out of the classroom wanting to run away from my beloved Okoboji. I was trapped this time. Me, giving a book report, in front of the whole class and Mr. Bemise.

I could not imagine having to actually go through with this assignment. He would have to give me a pass somehow. Mr. Bemise had to be aware that it was not possible for me to follow through with such an assignment. The month-long pressure building up to D-day would be unbearable. I went to see him after school.

"Am I g-g-going to have t-to d-do this?" I asked.

"Yes, Doug, you are," was his reply. "You can do it," he added.

"M-m-m-maybe y-y-you d-don't know about m-m-my p-p-problem."

"Yes, I know about your problem, but you will need to face this more and more from here on out in your life, and you may as well get started now," he explained.

I left the room in despair and with a dark foreboding future looking straight at me.

Our group selected works from Jack London, and I chose his *White Fang* for no other reason than the word "Fang" wasn't a problem for me to say. "White" was going to give me trouble, but in the whole scheme of things, it would be the least of my worries.

I read the book and was surprised how much I enjoyed it. Any reading other than comics was not a regular occurrence on my list of things to do in my leisure time. I took notes on what I was going to say and used words that might help me get through it.

We drew numbers out of a hat. Our group, thankfully, were to present our author to the class on Friday, and I was the last in my group to speak.

I paid attention to all the groups during the week to see if anything they did could aid me in my terrifying dilemma. The reports seemed easy enough for everyone to do. Class went on as usual; however, every day that went by was one day closer to my turn. Where were the mumps when I needed them?

It was finally Friday. I went through the motions in the other classes. Literature was in the afternoon. I ate lunch hoping I could keep it down.

It was time. The class had started, and our group took its place at the table in the front of the room. The other members of our group gave their reports one at a time. One was longer than usual, and I looked at the clock and did the math. Maybe time would run out. The next two were shorter than they were supposed to be. I was dead in the water; I would have to go through with my presentation for sure.

I never heard one word of what my group members said. Not one word. My heart was pounding in my ears, my mouth was dry, and my stomach was churning.

The group now turned the rest of the time over to me. Oh man oh man. I was afraid to look up. I was almost paralyzed. This was the very first time I'd have to perform verbally in a serious manner rather than with clown antics for an audience with so much on the line. I imagined everyone sitting on the edge of their seats waiting to break into riotous laughter, or worse, looking down at their shoes in preparation for the embarrassment that was about to unfold.

It was unfair on my part to accuse my classmates of any such reaction to my malady. We'd all been friends far too long, but giving a presentation of this magnitude was something new for me to do and something new for them to witness.

"Please, God, take me out of here. Strike me down," I prayed.

The seriousness of this situation now rested upon my shoulders. I would not be able to joke my way out of this one. It seemed in an instant of time all my past humiliations were coming back into focus to haunt me, to taunt me. I was drowning in terror and fear. My heart was pounding. My ears were buzzing and hot. My hands were icy cold. My mouth was dry. This moment had finally come down the conveyor belt. I had to begin to talk.

I slowly picked my words, "The book I chose was *White Fang*, by Jack London."

I hadn't tripped up on the word, White. It just came out for some unknown reason. The author's name managed to slip through as well.

I continued, "This is a story that begins in the freezing Yukon. It's about a part dog, part wolf that was turned into a fighting monster."

What was happening here? I actually said the mother of all stutter words, "Yukon," without skipping a beat. I began putting myself into the character of White Fang. He had had a hard life right from the get go. He had learned to survive. Death was always right around the next bend. Disaster always loomed in his future.

At this point, I was White Fang, struggling to survive. I was fighting for my life just as much as that troubled canine had to fight for his. I was now on the offensive, looking for disaster at every turn; in every sentence, in every word.

The words flowed from my more relaxed, but determined lips. The excitement was growing inside me as I unfolded the storyline. I stayed on target. I wasn't marveling at what was happening here; I was only following the pathway to the finish line. It was almost as if I was a dummy sitting on the lap of a ventriloquist. I finally had a glimpse, a sweet taste, of what life was like to be fluent. I didn't want the moment to end.

But end it did. I finished my report. My time was up. I laid my papers back onto the table and looked up at the kids. The teacher was smiling. He winked at me. The kids didn't seem to notice they had just witnessed a modern day miracle. The bell rang; the class was over.

Mr. Bemise handed each of us our grades after we were finished. He gave me, his disturbing element, an A+ and a comment of, "Great job, Doug!" My endorphins were off to the races.

———————

Let's jump ahead about six years: Unfortunately, not every presentation turned out like this. Once in a landscape design class in college, we were given the assignment to do a planting design for a small city park in Philadelphia. This vest-pocket park was located where a small building may have been demolished, and the city wanted to avoid a blighted situation. All the hardscape was given to us; the sidewalks, planting areas, raised planters, lighting, seating areas, and entryways. All we were assigned was the planting design. The department expected us to draw up a plan and a perspective view and present it to the entire landscape architecture class, together with grad students, professors, and heads of the department.

It was my sophomore year, and I had just declared my major but didn't know much about design or plant material. I was still unclear what the concept of design was. I had gone through life believing trees and shrubs were where they were because that's where they were, not because someone put any thought into a design that put them there.

We were expected to explain what plants we specified and why we used them. The deadline was a month away, and like most projects, I waited until the final week to knock it out. Not aware of any particular reasons for using one plant over another, I used all evergreen trees and shrubs instead of mixing them with some deciduous ones. I worked all night on the drawings and, to me, they looked pretty good. My drawing skills were way ahead of my design knowledge.

I wore a pressed good-looking ochre-colored pinstriped shirt and a solid blue tie. I walked to the LA (landscape architecture) building and found over a hundred people waiting for the presentations to commence. This was serious stuff; at least it was supposed to be.

Alphabetically, I was first up. I taped my large drawings to the wall. I was now about to come face to face with all those brochures telling me how important communicative skills would be in the field of landscape design.

I began by explaining why I used all evergreen plants. It was a lame explanation because to be honest, I didn't know enough about any other plants that would have been a better choice.

I was sweating profusely, and my ears were becoming hot again. I answered several questions the best I could, but always had to resort to using easier words to say when responding. Instead of using the word, "perimeter," a common design term, I used the phrase, "around the outside." I knew I would have stumbled on the "p" word. I certainly didn't want a blockage to knock me into stutter-hell.

Just when I thought I had managed to pull it off, a fellow classmate, Dave, asked me to clarify one point, "How do you get inside the park?"

Complete silence enveloped the room. Apparently, everyone in there had been asking themselves the same question, everyone but me.

I looked at the drawing. I had drawn white pines around the entire perimeter and left no space for access. This would be regarded as a huge faux pas. This would also be construed as not knowing "jack" about the world of design, and maybe I should seriously consider some other course of study. I knew why he asked me to explain. It was a valid question, too valid for me. It was all too apparent that I hadn't considered an entrance to the park. Again, I figured those little details just took care of themselves. I was finally beginning to discover what the word design meant; unfortunately, the revelation was unfolding in front of the whole LA department.

I looked at the drawing again, then at Dave, then out at the vast audience of future landscape designers and department professors. I looked at the Dean of the Department who was also my counselor. Every one of them knowing more about what they were doing than I obviously did.

They were all waiting for an answer. I was about to be exposed as an imposter. What could I say to get out of this situation and salvage any pride I might have left? What sort of trick did I have up my sleeve to save me this time? No funny, witty anecdote was going to pull me out this Pete's Pond.

I looked back at my drawings, ripped them off the wall, crumpled them in my hands, and while tossing them into the wastebasket on the way out, I responded, "You parachute in."

Hey, I was thinking, the world needs ditch diggers, too. Then there's always that candy apple gig to fall back on.

# CHAPTER SIXTEEN

# SATURDAY NIGHT FEVER

Junior high was when I made most of my friends, friends that I kept for a long time. When I was younger, kids moved in and out of my life all the time until they, eventually just became another face in the crowd.

I went to my first girl/boy party at thirteen. Sue Jensen was in my class and came up with the idea of an Orange Party. The lucky ones in the class who were invited were given an invitation with a drawing of an orange on the cover and the information inside. The orange part of it was just putting straws into an unpeeled orange and sucking out the juice. This was hardly worth top billing, but it could have been a cow-pie party, and I was still going to be there. After all, Sue was the head cheerleader in junior high, which meant I was being included in the in-crowd.

I found out rather quickly not to mention it to other friends, after doing just that to someone who wasn't invited. I was embarrassed that I'd brought it up. The hurt on his face was unmistakable even though he mentioned he had other plans that Saturday night. No one our age had plans on Saturday night in February in Iowa. It was normally just one more weekend night staying home drinking a bottle of Coke and watching *Gunsmoke* on television with the family.

The day of the party finally arrived after a long two-week wait for it. I had my pants and shirt all picked out. Mom ironed them for me. I took my bath early and got dressed. My hair was always an issue. For some reason, I adopted a style not easily maintained for extended periods of time.

I'd comb it while wet from back to front and then part it on both sides. Next, I'd comb the top of the parts toward the center and the bottom of the parts down. After all this I combed a pathway between the two top parts down to the front, adding a ski-jump above my forehead. The other kids thought it was cool, so I stayed with it. Dad hated it.

Mom was enjoying the excitement of my first party almost as much as I was. I had asked Mike if I could use a little of his English Leather aftershave lotion sitting on top of our dresser, so I smelled pretty good, too. Ted Swift had the best smell, though; he used his older brother's Jade East. In time, all the guys were slopping on that stuff.

Bill Enders and I walked over to Sue's and got there right on time. We weren't going to miss a minute of whatever was supposed to happen at an orange party.

The much-anticipated event was held in Sue's basement. It was decorated with orange streamers, the lights were low, and music was playing. Bobby Vee's, "Devil or Angel" must have played ten times throughout the evening. Of course, the boys were on one side of the room and the girls on the other.

The guys were acting like it didn't matter if the girls were there or not, but we were sneaking peeks to their side of the room every three seconds. This was between the back slapping and the scuffing of each other's shoes.

Some of the eighth-grade boys began to break the ice by asking their girlfriends to dance. We all stopped what we were doing and watched, not believing we could be that close to a girl by just asking her.

However, the idea of my walking over to the girl side of the room in full view of everyone and asking one of them to dance was off the humiliation chart. First of all, I didn't know how to dance. Good heavens, what if she said yes? Or worse, what if she said no? I couldn't very well move on down the line to second and then the third choice. If they took offense and all said no, I'd have to leave town.

Of course, there was always the likely chance that I might not be able to even ask them in the first place.

A possible scenario played out in my mind a hundred times, "D-D-Do y-y-y-you w-w-w-want t-t-to d-d-d-dance?"

Everyone on my side would be laughing at me and pointing while every girl there would be whispering to each other and, of course, snickering. It would have been tough to live that down. Safety in numbers by hanging with the guys might be the order of the day, and yet we were all feeling something different and powerful going on. There was no denying that.

Later on, after the orange-sucking refreshments were served, my attention was directed to a darker part of the basement, but not too dark. There had been an area set aside for couples who apparently already knew each other. There was a sofa just behind some streamers hanging from the ceiling, creating a space occupied at the moment by four kids in the eighth grade. One of the guys at the boy-wall told me to check it out. I had no idea what was going on. When I looked, I couldn't believe what I was seeing.

There they were, people I'd known for years, kissing each other ... a lot. We called it making out or necking. Even uttering those words would evoke deep emotions from a thirteen-year-old boy, especially one like me who had yet to experience a first kiss.

I was embarrassed to be standing there witnessing this display of affection, but stand there I did. I was wondering what Frank and Willie might do if they caught me glaring at them. About that time Frank came up for air, discovered my apparent curiosity, smiled and waved before starting up his lips again. I assumed he was putting on a show at this point, but I still felt like a weird peeping Tom, which, to be truthful, I guess I was. I walked back to the boy-wall, but I wasn't interested in scuffing anyone's shoes anymore. After all, people were making out just around the corner.

The next Monday after school, Mom asked me to sit down and talk with her. She said she had heard that four kids were kissing in full view of everyone at Sue's party. I was too mortified to speak. I couldn't talk to my mom about something like this. She said she was disappointed it had happened, and she would make sure it didn't happen again at any other parties I might be invited to. I was relieved she didn't bring up the fact that I was one of the goons watching. I didn't want her to know I liked girls.

In the spring, I decided to host a Garage Party. We had a huge garage. Since May was always a great month for weather, that's when I scheduled it. My dad used to work for a meat packing company headquartered in Fort Dodge, Iowa. He had a regular route and drove a refrigerated truck all over the state selling his products to customers.

He built a heated garage large enough to house the truck so it would start on those brutal frozen winter mornings. The garage had a standard commercial height door for the truck and a regular one for his beloved 1959 Desoto station wagon. It was a massive garage, as far as garages go, one that I would have to paint with a brush by myself when I was fourteen.

Dad had changed jobs by the time he bought the Chris Craft boat, so he stored the boat on the truck side of the garage during the off season. Mike took it upon himself to refinish the hull by sanding, varnishing and painting the bottom while it was in dry dock. He even went to the trouble of refilling all the hardware screw holes with toothpicks and glue to be able to re-tighten the hatches. I admired him for taking on that project. To this day, I'm not sure why I wasn't asked to help him. When he finished, it looked like a new boat again. Dad was proud of him and took all his friends out to the garage to show them what Mike had accomplished.

By this time the boat had already been launched for the upcoming season, so the garage was open for a party. I wanted my party to be a success, as anyone giving a party does, but first, I had to clean the place. I moved everything outside that wasn't nailed down and hosed the concrete floor. The garage hadn't been that clean since it was new. I hung streamers, and Dad brought his treasured Magnavox stereo out and set it up.

Dad also offered his suggestions on how to throw a great party. "What you should do," he offered, "is blow up a bunch of balloons with all the names of the girls inside, hoist them up to the ceiling in a big sheet, and tie them off. Then, at ten o'clock, release them. The boys then dance with the girl whose name was in their balloon."

"I d-d-don't think so, Dad," I replied. "M-Most of the guys wouldn't w-w-want someone else d-d-dancing with their g-g-girl."

"Oh, that's just plain stupid. It's not like they're married. Everyone will go away saying, 'Man, that Doug Andersen sure knows how to throw a great party,'" he insisted.

"I don't th-think so," I argued, "kids aren't l-l-like that t-t-today. Do I have to?"

"Do what you want; I'm just trying to help you have a good time, that's all," he fired back.

He was attempting to help. I just didn't want to spend that much time blowing up balloons and wondering how to get them all the way up to the twenty-foot ceiling. I figured low lights and a make-out bench would be pretty much all I would need. I was still thinking about recreating that first party atmosphere that was still floating around in my mind. I wasn't even too worried about how Mom might react. I'd worry about that later.

A couple of the more popular girls came over during the day to check out my hard work. They wore their dads' white dress shirts, tails out, and had their hair up in curlers. It reassured me that maybe I was going to be able to pull this off.

The last thing I did was drag in our five-foot long wooden sofa swing. I had it set up where the smaller garage door was. I hung streamers down from the wheel tracks forming a sort of love room. It was right out in the open and was avoided like the plague. I discovered it's almost impossible to recreate that magical first impression, and it embarrassed me that I had even tried. I guess the word got out with the parents.

Everyone attended the party that I hoped would come. We danced to the familiar tunes of the other parties, so nothing much changed except the venue. Since I didn't have any records of my own, I had to borrow from other kids. Records were a dollar apiece for the 45-speed ones, and I didn't see the value of purchasing them yet. I did try to play some of Dad's records that I had grown to like. I mistakenly thought my friends would like them as much as I did. Some Ray Conniff Singers, Andy Williams, and Tony Bennet, but the kids complained and called me a weirdo. So I went back to playing "Devil or Angel" by Bobbie Vee. It seemed every hit record then was sung by someone named Bobbie or Frankie.

Everyone seemed to have a good time so, all in all, it was a successful party by seventh grade standards. I wasn't aware of how uninvited guests would treat me after the event. Like I've stated, I knew all these kids since kindergarten. Looking back, I wish I would have invited the entire junior high class or at least most of them. It was the only party I ever hosted.

The first record I bought was Gene Pitney's, "Liberty Valance." I had to make a choice between that or Chubby Checker's, "The Twist." Since the ballads have always intrigued me, it wasn't much of a choice. The two guys with me tried to sway me the other way to the point of ridicule, but I knew what I liked. I prized that first musical purchase. I would flip the play switch on my dad's Magnavox, run out to the back patio, sit in a chair, and listen to it for the two and one-half minutes it would play. Then I'd run back inside and flip the switch again, repeating this process until someone in the house complained. Both Dad and Mom were disappointed that I had made a turn in my musical tastes. Dad especially hated the Four Seasons,' "Big Girls Don't Cry." He'd mimic Frankie Valley's screeching falsetto directly in my face thinking, apparently, that this would somehow help me see the light.

The second record I laid down a dollar for was Johnny Crawford's (Marcus McCain of The Rifleman fame), "Your Nose is Going to Grow" with the flipside being "Mr. Blue." Hey, Jimmy Hendrix hadn't recorded anything yet.

Susie Phelps had a basement party a few months prior to my party. Peggy Smart was there with brand new braces on her teeth. By this time the guys were more emboldened than before, even me, and I asked Peggy to dance several times. Each time after the short dance, I would then escort her to the girl-wall, only to walk over there again and ask her to dance when a new song started. I was not up to the task of starting a conversation with her between dances.

With three-minute songs, it got awkward. In the past three years, I still had never spoken ten sentences to her when I wasn't wearing a dress. She asked me what I thought of her new dental work to which I replied, "You're going to have a w-w-wonderful smile, Peggy." Apparently, she liked what I said. The next day I heard she liked me again. It was time to go into my wave and run mode.

A few of us who had been to the party were talking about it at the drug store the next day. Tad Olson, who was a year older, mentioned to me, "Doug, I just can't figure out what Peggy sees in you."

I tried to ignore it even when everyone else heard him. I was standing by the booth; he was sitting.

Wondering if I had heard him, he said again, a little louder this time, "I don't understand why she likes you."

How does one comment on such a statement? I just walked off with my ears burning.

I wondered why Tad was interested in what Peggy liked or didn't like.

Silly me; Tad and Peggy have been married for over forty years.

# CHAPTER SEVENTEEN

# WASTED TALENT

Junior high was when I met Bob Baker. I'm not sure where he came from; I just know he showed up on the scene in Spirit Lake one day when we were both about twelve. He had an impressive chrome Schwinn three-speed bicycle and a huge paper route binder hanging from the handle bars. Back then we paperboys were measured somewhat by the size of our binder rings which held the weekly receipt stubs for Friday's collection day. I was never in the running, but Bob's was one of the biggest in town. I first met him at the local Snow White, an ice cream cone place. He bought me a fifteen-cent hot dog. No one but my parents had ever bought me a hot dog before.

He had a guitar and a typewriter at home that he had purchased with his own money. Who was this guy? He wore a pair of Buddy Holly heavy black horn-rimmed glasses and had the waviest red hair I'd ever seen on a human. He was always laughing; it was a devious one. It was a laugh that made people wonder if they'd missed the joke; maybe one about to be played on them. Everyone liked Bob because he tried so darn hard to be likable.

His father owned a furniture store in town where Bob worked at sales and delivery when he was old enough. He had the gift of gab to be sure and learned the art of the sale rapidly. Farmers were buying sofas when they came in looking for a lamp shade. He could have succeeded at anything he put his mind to.

One of his shining moments was when he played Captain Von Trapp in *The Sound of Music* opposite Peggy Smart as Maria and got to kiss her in front of the whole town. Two performances, one dress rehearsal, and who knows how many other rehearsals were counted in my mind to determine just how many times he kissed her. Even though he was my best friend, and by then we'd been through so much together, all that kissing business was still hard for me to watch or think about. I was relieved when the play was finished.

Bob's birthday was in late August. He was the last one in the class to get his driver's license. He hated being the youngest in our class; however, when he did get his license he bought himself a 1963 white Ford Galaxy convertible with black bucket seats and a floor shifter. It was more than beautiful. He had saved up his money, fifteen hundred dollars, and paid for it himself. There was no stopping him now. He was free to explore at will. One year he stood in line for hours in his attempt to acquire the license plate with sixty-nine stamped on it. Back then you were issued a number coinciding with the order in which a driver picked up his new plate. He misjudged and got seventy instead. It was a major disappointment for him to bear. In the next couple of years, we spent endless summer nights singing along with the Beatles' *Sgt. Pepper* album.

He attended the University of Iowa while I chose Iowa State, so we saw each other less often during those years, but we still spent a lot of time together during the summers in Okoboji. Ever the life of any party, he kept falling behind in his studies and dropping classes. As the years went by, most of us were finally figuring out school and advancing with the program, but not Bob.

He left Iowa one fall to enroll at Glendale Community College in Arizona. Due to a broken arm mishap, I had to leave Iowa State for a semester, so I followed him down to Phoenix in December of 1969. He was living with a bunch of guys that didn't have jobs as far as I could tell. Being true to form, he had already dropped out of his new college. Playing the responsible straight man, I insisted we apply for some kind of work at the unemployment office. He complied, and the next day we were hired on as "gophers" for a Hollywood television company. It was a case of being in the right place at exactly the right time.

Our only qualifications were to be in possession of a driver's license and having knowledge of the Phoenix area. Bob had lived here for twelve weeks. I'd been in Phoenix for twelve hours. When we met with Mr. Katz, the production manager, Bob convinced him we were exactly what he was looking for. I didn't say a word.

A gopher is someone on hand to go-for anything needed on the movie set. This production company was filming a new TV show entitled *Something Else* and was hosted by the comedian, John Byner. The premise of the show was to highlight a different popular artist or group each week in a natural surrounding instead of a studio.

My first assignment was to drive a U-Haul truck to Wickenburg and pick up all the dancing girls' costumes. Wickenburg had several dude ranches. The Turtles were booked there for a week and were to sing their big hit, "Happy Together" while riding a horse through a desert wash. Production shooting went over the allotted time because some of the members of the band were too drunk to stay in the saddle. I guess they were too happy together. I was sorry I'd missed the show.

When I arrived everyone was eating dinner at picnic tables in a large room. I happened to find an empty seat directly across the table from Mr. Byner. He politely stood up and introduced himself to me, as if he needed to. I'd been a fan of his for years from the *Johnny Carson* show. He was one of the funniest men on the planet.

They had scheduled the Beach Boys to sing at a water park in Tempe, called Big Surf. I was looking forward to that to be sure, only to have the park's wave-making machine break down and canceling the group's performance. They substituted Billy J. Royal and his, "Down in the Boondocks" hit. Compared to the Beach Boys, this really was down in the boondocks.

This job lasted for three amazing weeks with too many stories to list here. Eventually, we drove home to Iowa in Bob's Ford convertible which had seen better days by now. We sang with the new Beatles' album, *Abby Road*, all thirteen hundred miles playing on his eight-track tape machine. We arrived just after the New Year, just in time to attend my brother's wedding.

Bob eventually dropped out of the University of Iowa for good and moved back home, taking some worthless classes at a local community college, where he and I would hook up whenever I got home on breaks. We'd sing the new Beatles' *White Album* together until dawn.

By the time I was a junior in college, I think he was still a freshman. One year Bob took a summer off from working at his father's store and traveled around the country hitchhiking with a dog he found somewhere; almost as if he was looking for answers. His constant lagging behind his peers, at least in academics, I believe may have been weighing on his mind a great deal.

Bob could have taken over his dad's store and had a remarkable life in Okoboji, but to him, that was a form of surrendering. He was too proud to stay in his little Podunk hometown. There was almost a stigma associated with hanging around little Spirit Lake, and not getting out into the real world. Gee, what nonsense that was. Many of us suffered from that same delusional misguidance.

The next year, after his wandering trek, while home for winter break, I got a call from his dad. He said when Bob was on some sort of LSD trip, he put a knife into his chest. He died instantly. I was stunned. I didn't know exactly how to react, how to process the material. I didn't cry or wail. I went straight over to my Dad's place of work, he had just hung up the phone with the news from Mom. He looked at me and shook his head. Words were not needed and weren't rendered.

Bob's parents were crushed and were saying it had been a terrible drug-induced accident, not suicide. I concurred with them but wasn't privately convinced.

That would have been a terribly confusing way to die. LSD must be strange enough to experience by itself, but then to give up the ghost while this drug has you in its clutches, would've been most bewildering to Bob or anyone. I've often wondered what thoughts entered his mind when that knife entered his heart.

From what is written concerning near-death experiences, the departed's realization of actually being dead doesn't necessarily have to happen simultaneously with the event itself. Like I said, it was probably a most confusing event.

This was truly a tragedy. He was the sort of fellow who naturally drew instant curiosity from others. Who would he marry? What kind of father would he be? Where would he open his next furniture store?

Twenty-one was far too young for pallbearer duty.

# CHAPTER EIGHTEEN

# CRASH GORDON

Turning sixteen was almost as important as being born. It was an absolute right of passage that had no equal in a kid's life. This age coincides with the number of years we must walk the earth before we are allowed to drive the earth.

In Iowa, permits to learn to drive were available at fourteen, which meant we were permitted to operate a vehicle with a parent. It was always a double-take to see classmates I knew most of my life, who just happened to be a few months older than I seated behind the steering wheel. They'd be driving down the road with their parent sitting on what seemed like the wrong side of the front seat. It was even more disturbing if it was a girl.

As more and more of my fellow classmates began falling into that privileged category of legal drivability, it became a waiting game for everyone else. My birthday fell in early February, so I was in the older half of my class. Some had to wait until late summer, and everyone felt their pain.

The driver's license examiner came to our small town on Fridays, which just happened to be smack-dab on my fourteenth birthday. Had it been one day later, on Saturday, I would have to wait until the next week to take the learner's exam, but as usual, my stars were aligned. On my birthday, I could run down there and pass this thing. Then I'd announce to my parents they needn't be burdened with driving anymore, I was there to take that task away from them.

I studied the booklet like I should have studied my class subjects. I was ready. The man gave me my test sheet, and I began marking circles.

Who would've known they were actually serious about memorizing stopping distances at various speeds? To me, sixty feet was the same as thirty feet where skid marks are concerned. And what's the big deal about knowing all the speed limits in conjunction with school zones, business districts, residential streets, and highways? Wasn't that what speed limit signs were for? One week later I passed the test on the second try, by the narrowest of margins.

Mom would allow me to drive if she wasn't in much of a hurry. She heard the now oft spoken phrase, "Can I drive?" on the way to the car, and it soon became annoying to her. Why else would I want to accompany her when she took my sister Marcia to her piano lesson? I seldom asked Dad.

Once in Spencer, Dad asked if I'd like to drive home, about twenty miles, a night drive. I was flabbergasted. I must have had a recent good report card.

I made every move slowly and correctly. I was dimming my headlights whenever an oncoming car approached. I was on my best driving behavior. When we arrived, he complimented me on my fine job. This was no small deal, still remembering it over fifty years later.

My sixteenth birthday fell on a Monday. The examiner wouldn't be there until Friday. It was like watching a clock. I had studied my stopping distances and school zone speeds. I had been forced to watch many of my classmates driving alone in their cars; they waved to me. They looked so grown-up, except the short ones; they looked out of place and probably always would. Just a few more days and I would know what unadulterated freedom was all about, too.

Of course, all that freedom could be snatched away in an instant due to a recently passed law regarding new drivers. The newer Iowa law stated that if a violation occurred in the first year of driving (for teens), the license would be suspended for thirty days, sixty to ninety days if an accident was involved. Of course, that was never going to happen to me. Unthinkable events like that only happened to the less fortunate.

In November, Ted Swift got his license. Tom Hagerty, Bill Thomas, and I all drove down to Spencer with Ted on a Saturday afternoon. We all chipped in fifty cents for gas. It was the first time any of us had driven there without supervision, and we were all feeling good about ourselves. We were all grown-up and harvesting the fruits of our newly acquired or soon to be acquired rites of passage.

Spencer had this poor excuse for an indoor mall. It housed a JC Penny's, a small drug store, a grocery store, a sporting goods store, and men's store. We walked around for about an hour, bought some cashews and a coke and looked forward to the ride home. We were almost there when Ted took a downhill turn a little too fast on an icy road and ended up sliding into the bumper of an approaching pickup. Minimal damage resulted to either vehicle, but we all knew what it meant for Ted. He was going to lose his license for at least a month, probably two.

All the fun and excitement of the day's journey came to a screeching halt. He choked up when we continued the journey home, surprising me. Ted was a football and basketball star in our school; it was strange to see him reacting this way. He was the kid who pinned me in a junior high wrestling tournament in gym class. I felt sorry for Ted, but at the same time, I was thinking this sort of thing was never going to happen to me. Even having witnessed an accident first hand, and it was my first, the prospect of my being responsible for a mishap was still inconceivable.

Friday, my examination day finally came, and it was snowing quite heavily. The superintendent even announced a school snow day. Worried that maybe the traveling officer wouldn't show up, I went to the city hall around ten o'clock in the morning to find out. He was there, and I passed the written test, again, with little room to spare. The officer got into the passenger seat of my Dad's new yellow 1964 Buick Special to begin the driving portion of the exam.

This Buick was the only new car I can remember Dad owning while I lived there. It wasn't a big lumbering car like an Oldsmobile or Mercury but seemed light weight and easy to drive, quite responsive. Mom and I, and my sister Marcia, who would be driving next year, were supposed to use this car and leave his Desoto station wagon alone.

Dad had a love affair with that Desoto. The interior had just been refurbished with carpeting and newly upholstered seats. New creamy-white paint and body work on the exterior along with white wall tires completed the transformation of Dad's 1959 Desoto to near new condition. It had only been a couple of weeks since the work was finished. He loved that station wagon in large part because it had a push button transmission. He was a Chrysler man through and through. The distinct sound of that starter motor every morning was pure Chrysler/ Plymouth.

Lots of snow had accumulated on the ground during the night, but the skies were clearing. The plows had been running non-stop for ten hours, so Main Street was beginning to be drivable. I was performing my driving skills the best I could even though the snow was still covering most of the street striping. The officer mentioned how great the car handled in the deep snow and how well I was doing in spite of all the mess. He skipped the parallel parking exercise because he thought for sure we'd get stuck doing it. I was disappointed a little because I had learned that move well in driver's education the summer before. He told me to drive back to the police station, where he would give me my ticket to heaven. The second part of my life, the important part, was now about to commence.

A couple of weeks later a friend of mine had a small get-together at his house on West Okoboji. His parents' home was big and beautiful. Four of my friends and I brought dates. I brought Peggy Smart; it was the first and only date with her or anyone else in my graduating class I would ever have. It was a low-key event; quiet music, subdued lighting, and simple conversation. I left most of the talking to everyone else, not wanting to spoil this fairy tale moment. I felt adult just being there; we all did. We left after a couple of hours, and I drove her home. I kissed her for the first and last time. I'm sure both of us wondered what that would be like after so many years of testing the waters. Turning sixteen was just like it was supposed to be. Everything was right with the world. However, dark clouds were forming on the horizon.

The next week Mom asked me to run down to the store and get some bread and lettuce. It was around five o'clock in the afternoon and already dark. I could have made it there in less than two minutes on foot. I'd done it a thousand times. It was only a block away; however, now that I was driving, I had no reason to walk anywhere as long as a car was available, and one was. Dad's cherished Desoto was sitting in the garage.

Dad had taken the Buick to work that day to have the oil changed for free in the garage at Stoller's where a full-time mechanic staff serviced all the smelly old fish trucks. Since the keys were always left in the ignition in those days, all I had to do was hop in, start it up, and back out. Life couldn't get any better.

After running the errand for Mom, I decided to take a detour on the way home via the lake route. Almost to Big Spirit Lake, I wondered what Dad's Desoto would do if I floored the accelerator for a split second. This car had a big engine, and I'd been told by friends that it could probably lay rubber even while in motion. This move could not have been more ill-timed.

A snowpack had blanketed the road, turning it into what's known as "black ice." When I slammed the accelerator down to the floor, the rear tires spun, the front of the car shifted to the right, and I lost all control. The car hit a large electrical pole snapping it in two. The loud, sickening sound was reminiscent of a bad dream. This couldn't be happening to me. I led a charmed life. I'd wake up soon and learn from it. Meanwhile, my accident was still in progress.

The Desoto catapulted onto the frozen lake adjacent to the road while turning in slow motion. Huge explosive metal to metal crash sounds with busting glass filled the interior of the car. I noticed the movement of the seats and the dashboard. I had absolutely no fear for my life during all this, only fear of facing Dad. The car flipped twice and landed upside-down on the foot-thick ice. Except for the radiator hissing, it was quiet again. Had it been April, I would have drowned.

Stunned and lying on the ceiling of the car, I crawled out of a now broken window and looked around at what I had done. This was no dream. I had completely destroyed my dad's beloved Desoto station wagon. I would not be waking up, relieved the nightmare was over. My charmed life motto had betrayed me. I realized that I was no more protected from evil or sadness, or accidents than anyone else. In fact, I was more susceptible to all this due to my cavalier attitude when it came to responsibility. I was my own worst enemy.

In total shock and somewhat denial, I walked off the ice and up the embankment to the road. Even in the dark, I could see the spaghetti of black downed power lines lying all over the snowy ground. I avoided them, but not as carefully as I should have. Somehow, it didn't seem all that imperitive to have survived the accident. How was I going to explain this to my dad?

One of my friends, who happened to live out on the lake stopped to see if anyone was hurt, then went to his home and called the police.

The police car pulled up after a few minutes, and Butch Busby, my neighbor, asked me to get into the back seat. The last time I had to deal with him was when I threw a rock at a bird, and it hit his windshield; that and the water tower incident. I told him the car hit an ice patch, and I lost control, leaving out the part about how I was wondering what the Desoto would do if I floored it for a split second.

Butch left, and I was alone in the car, not daring to look up at the carnage I had caused. A crowd gathered with everyone dressed in parkas, hats, and gloves. No one had bothered to turn off their engines or headlights, so they could return home in a warm car. Everyone was pointing and talking with steam floating out of their mouths with each breath. The wrecker arrived and added his yellow spinning lights to Butch's patrol car's red spinning ones. The man assessed the situation on how best to bring the now mangled Desoto off the ice in one piece. By now everyone knew whose car was out there on its top, exposing its ugly underside, and who had been driving. My fantasy world had come to an end, and I hadn't even faced Dad yet. If I could only have that instant back again. Just this one time, please.

The door beside me opened; it was Dad. He got in and sat beside me. He asked if I was alright. I told him yes. He asked why I was driving his car to the store. I told him I didn't know. Later, we drove home in the Buick, a car I would never drive again.

The next day he took me to where they had towed the car. He wanted me to have a good look at it in the daylight. He informed me that since I was supposed to have been driving only the Buick, he didn't have collision insurance on the Desoto. He told me it was a total loss except for the $150 he got for the push button transmission. He wanted me to know that the wreckage part was certainly my fault, but the lack of insurance wasn't. Still, I wanted to crawl into a hole and die. Dad didn't say another word about it; not the accident, not the loss, not anything until the unthinkable happened the following week. A perfect storm was brewing again for me.

Later that night, the Okoboji area had the worst snowstorm anyone alive had ever seen. The cold black skies dumped at least four feet of snow, which made for snow drifts up to twenty feet high. When this happened everything came to a halt until the plows began the seemingly hopeless task of opening the roads.

The skies were clear by morning; it was snow shoveling time for me. The schools were closed for several days. The buses were snowed in. I was glad I had something to take the accident off my mind for a while. If I was ever going to drive again, I would have to use my own car which I would have to pay for myself. Shoveling snow was a start in that direction.

It was a Tuesday night, six days after my accident. Schools had been reopened, and a volleyball tournament was held at the high school. I went there with Dean Nevel. He had a beautiful two-door 1961 powder blue Chevy Impala with baby moon hubcaps. Around nine-thirty in the evening we left the high school for home. Dean had been dating Wendy for a while and wanted to spend a little kissing time with her in the back seat while I drove us to her house.

On the way out to his car, he handed me his keys and made it clear who was driving. I was surprised and delighted to accommodate him. I figured I wouldn't be behind the wheel of a car for several months or more depending on future job prospects, of which I had none.

---

In my defence, let me offer a lame excuse for what's about to happen: After a snowstorm like the one we had a week prior, all the city could do was make drivable pathways throughout the town. The snow was so high it even covered all the stop signs. Every automobile had an extended antenna about ten feet high with a flag attached to the top to be seen at intersections. It was similar to driving around in a giant maze. The snow out on the road around Big Spirit Lake had drifted to twenty-five feet high. A couple of days later they brought in huge snow blowers from South Dakota to eat away at the cold white stuff. We watched those monster machines work in tandem slowly inching forward while blowing out brilliant white snow thirty feet in the air which landed a hundred feet away against a vivid blue frigid sky. It was a sight to behold.

---

So, I was driving slowly and carefully, knowing Dean was close by and had trusted me, for some reason, to do this. As I came up to an intersection, I could see a glowing light appear on the snowbank on the far side. A car was coming my way from the right so I applied the brakes. The streets were still snow packed from a week's worth of traffic, and they provided no friction whatsoever for stopping. Again, like in slow motion and out of control, I gently slid into the side of the lady's car, pushing it into the far snow bank. Even after impact, Dean's car continued forward and slammed into her car again, making sure we had maximum damage.

Dean shot up from the backseat, not expecting anything too extensive due to the relatively quiet crash noise, but when we stood outside looking down at the wreckage, he knew differently. I had just destroyed three cars in less than a week. Was my nightmare ever going to end? Someone called the police from a neighbor's phone. Butch Busby was again on duty, and Dean, Wendy, and I got into his back seat when he arrived. Butch finally climbed into his driver's seat.

He knew the car was Dean's. Everybody knows everyone's car in small towns, especially the police. He asked Dean how it happened as he was writing on a pad. Dean pointed in my direction.

He turned around, looked at me, and asked, "Andersen, are you still driving?"

With my sullen face buried in my hands, I replied softly, "Not anymore, Butch, not anymore."

How could I even go home after this? How could I show my face in school? Apparently, I needed two accidents in rapid succession to finally convince me that I was not protected by an unseen force in any way. I was going to be screwed like anyone else who didn't have the intelligence or the inclination to think things through. I needed some serious downtime in the driving department.

The State of Iowa felt the same way.

Butch took me back to the station about ten-thirty that night. I had some forms to fill out. Butch was a good guy, a huge man, and he genuinely liked me, but I knew he was glad I wasn't his son. He asked if I wanted a lift home. I told him no thanks. Was I even going home? Of course, there were no other options, but why hurry it up with a ride?

The late night walk home was deafeningly quiet. The only sound I could hear was my shoes crunching on the snowy street, reminding me of my paper route days. I turned the corner and walked up the street to the house. I opened the door and walked in. Mom was still up, sitting on the couch reading, with Dad's head in her lap. He was sleeping. Mom looked at me with sorrowful knowing eyes and asked, "What happened?"

"I wrecked Dean's car," was my doleful reply.

Dad came flying off the couch, "You did what?"

He slapped my face so hard I fell down. I should have stayed down, but I figured I deserved all I was about to get. I don't remember anything he said; my ears were ringing from the several blows I was receiving.

Some of my friends told me over the years how they actually had fist fights with their fathers or at least learned how to defend themselves against an onslaught like this. I would listen and marvel how foreign that was to me. I never even referred to my dad as "my old man". Every kid I knew called their father that, some even to their face. To me, it was disrespectful. I just couldn't do it, and I never did; not one single time.

Dad's anger was probably an overflow from the loss of his Desoto and my bone-headed decision to drive one block to the store; couple that with this accident and something had to snap. Mom started crying and Dad finally stopped. My life was in the toilet. How could I feel any worse than I did at that moment? At school, my friends and the whole student body took care of that.

My name changed from Doug to Crash Gordon overnight. Every time I heard it, I winced. The State of Iowa sent me a letter one month after the accident. The letter stated that due to my driving record, they were suspending my license for one year starting in thirty days from the date of the letter.

I had been in possession of this driving privilege for one lousy month. It had turned my life into hell and sadness both at home and school. Why wait thirty days? I certainly wouldn't be driving. I put my license into the return envelope, walked down to the mailbox at the bottom of the hill, and opened the swinging door at the top. I looked at the letter for a few moments, then let it drop. I wouldn't be driving again until May of my junior year. The worst part would be hitching rides all summer in Okoboji one more time. I'd be missing the best part of my sixteenth golden summer.

Dad had to buy anything he could afford to replace the Desoto, which turned out to be a 1959 Oldsmobile Ninety-eight with a big engine. It was in pretty rough shape and needed a new muffler. A foreboding, melancholy-like cloud engulfed me whenever I heard it coming down the road, knowing full well everyone in town knew I was the reason he was driving it.

A year or so later he purchased a beautiful used Chrysler Imperial Crown Coupe. This car had the thickest, most comfortable leather seats I'd ever seen. This was his first automobile with leather seats. I never asked my dad about finances, so I had no idea how he came to buy this beauty. He had one of the truck mechanics at Stollers install a contraption called a Kar Bar in this beast. What a concept that was. This silly invention summoned any liquid the owner may have stored in his trunk right into your glass at the touch of a button which was mounted under the dashboard. Tort lawyers loved that sort of stuff.

My sister Marcia was now driving this car, and it was killing me. Everyone was driving except me, even underclassmen, which was the ultimate salt in the wound. Bob Baker got his license in late August and even offered me his car to drive if I wanted to. He was crazy like that, and his wonderful Ford Galaxy convertible with bucket seats was tempting, but I declined. During my entire suspension time, which turned out to be over fourteen months, I didn't drive one foot. Maybe I lacked in common sense, but at least I had respect for my father and the law.

I started working after school at Dad's plant, Stoller Fisheries. I worked as much as I could, going in on Saturdays as well, logging in ten or more hours that day. This place was known to attract men down on their luck, and I got to know some strange and scary people. My dad worked in the office and was in sales, mostly frozen fish. I worked on the cutting floor with some ex-cons who carried fillet knives and fish-head lopping cleavers.

Even though Dad was an employee himself, he was considered one of the bosses by most of the guys back there, so I felt relatively safe. Nonetheless, some of these men would look at me with wild eyes, which kept me on my toes most of the time.

I started out by cutting off the heads of dead fresh carp and sending them over to the fillet people. Of course, they called them, "fill-etts" instead of "fill-A's," but no one was keeping score on their French-speaking capabilities.

Although carp is defined as a trash fish, it was sold back east as "Okoboji Salmon." Of course, the buyer's knew it was carp, but they bought it anyway in thirty-pound tins, filleted and skinned. Maybe it substituted for white fish.

Later, I advanced, if one could call it that, to the fillet line, a skill I would use the rest of my life since I love fishing. We stood there for hours in the same spot cutting and smelling carp. We'd drop the fillets into a wire basket, and send them to the skinning machine, which I operated more times than I'd like to remember.

All the heads, racks, skins, and guts went into old 55-gallon drums standing beside us. Once filled, they were stored in an old cooler that had been converted into a slow cooking hot room to break down the mess. This room held about one hundred barrels of slime.

After about a week in there, the barrels were dumped into an auger trough that led to a fish meal plant in the next room. This process dried and powdered the stuff into mink food. Fish oil was a by-product which was stored in a huge tank outside. Another by-product of this operation was an odor no one wanted in their town. Stollers always had run-ins with the city about the smell. I'm sure the planning department cursed the day they let him build it in the first place, but then the joint did provide much-needed work for otherwise unemployable people.

Getting the drums to the auger was one of my jobs. I'd tip a drum onto a hand truck, wheel it out, dump it onto the floor, then shovel it into the trough. The drums weighed three to four hundred pounds each. After a long day, it became much harder to control these slimy barrels of slop. Just walking into the hot room with all the disgusting goo cooking away was more than some workers could take. Vomiting all over the place only improved the smell.

The metal drums were old beaten-up ones with holes on the sides and bottoms so blood and goo would seep out and gather on the floor, making it slippery and dangerous. Safety in the workplace was not a high priority at this plant in those days; it was never an issue. Several times I slipped, tipping the gut-filled drum contents all over me. That would garner a loud applause along with laughter from all the felons. The boss's snot-nosed kid just got slimed. There wasn't much else in that place to laugh about.

I was working and biding my time, waiting for May to come around again so I could reclaim my driver's license. When I did, I discovered I was on the expensive insurance plan. Not only was the price inflated, but I would be paying for it myself; a hefty sum of seventy-five dollars every three months. No matter, I went down to the

Ford dealership in town and bought a blue 1959 Chevy Impala four-door hardtop for $500.

When I got my license back from the officer, I immediately drove out to the scene of the first accident and waved at the new power pole as I passed by. "Monday Monday," by The Mommas & the Papas was playing on the radio. I was cautiously beginning to allow some hope and sunshine back into my life. I was finally emerging out of the long cold winter.

Dad liked my car, but not the way I was treating it. He had a valid point because I was less than responsible concerning its upkeep. As long as it was clean and had gas, I figured I was good to go.

Dad suspected as much, and he invited me out to check the oil in the engine. I didn't want to go through with this because he'd cautioned me about checking the engine oil in the past and it had been a long time since I had. He raised the hood and pulled out the dipstick, which was a term I was pretty much applying to myself at the moment. I watched as he wiped off the wire stick and re-inserted it back into the hole.

I was hoping for a miracle that I knew was not going to happen unless there was an oil fairy who filled crankcases at night. He pulled it out again only to find it dry as a bone.

"Doug," he yelled, "why in the hell don't you care about this engine? It was such a smooth running little engine when you got it. Why don't you at least check the damned oil level?"

I couldn't resist it. I responded, "B-b-because if I do, I'll know it n-n-needs oil, then I'll have to b-b-buy some."

He didn't say anything more. He just slammed down the hood and walked away.

I really was a dip stick.

I wish I could report that I had learned some surefire lessons in driving and that I had morphed into a responsible, careful driver, as a result, but, alas, I can't.

Pulling into the high school parking lot one snowy day with my sister Marcia, I failed to take notice of the slick asphalt. While navigating a parking spot, I rammed into the side of a classmate's 1952 Chevy. My sister said she'd never ride with me again. Of course, this tidbit of news spread like wildfire, and everyone knew that Crash Gordon was back in action.

The owner, a kid I knew, took it to Buck's Auto Shop for repairs. I would be paying cash since I could never afford to turn this into my insurance people. I was already on a tight leash with them.

I stopped by after school the next day, to see what the damages were going to amount to. Buck showed me the itemized costs. The items such as putty, paint, and tape came to only about thirty-five dollars. I was feeling so much better than I had been for two days, then he got out his little book telling him how much time he would need to spend to get this green relic back into shape. The total cost was going to be over one hundred and seventy-five dollars.

My stomach turned. Between my car payment and expensive insurance, this was going to wipe me out. The following week he called me and told me the car was ready, and he needed to be paid. I'd known Buck for several years since he moved to town and into the apartment over the auto shop with his family. His son was in my class, a real car buff. I knew he was giving me any breaks he could, but work is work and fair is fair.

I went to the bank and withdrew all my savings in cash. I walked into his garage, with knots in my stomach, took the money out of my pocket. He extended his hand, and while he was expressing sorrow for having to accept it, I crumpled the bills into a sweaty wad of money and gave it to him. It was not out of disrespect or malice, just a reaction coming from deep within me. This ball of money represented many hours of slipping in fish slime. I was bitterly angry with myself for having been so careless. This avoidable accident cost me all my savings. I expressed my sincere regrets for treating him this way. I meant no disrespect. I think he believed me.

I dated a girl for a while, Linda Stevenson, from the little farm town of Everly, located some forty miles to the southwest of Spirit Lake. I used to see her at Arnolds Park, jumping on the trampolines in her bathing suit years before. I remembered the suit. Her father, a heck of a guy, owned an RV park on East Okoboji Lake. Sometimes I'd stop by and see him when I was boating around.

Linda and I were on our way to my high school's homecoming football game. That meant a long ride to her house and a long ride to the school, only to do it all over again before the evening was over. With a hundred and sixty miles to drive in one night, it's easy to drive over the posted speed limit of sixty mph. The roads in Iowa are mostly elevated asphalt, two-lane ribbons, called blacktops. I was traveling north with Linda at ninety miles an hour on a flat dry surface.

My attention was momentarily focused on my radio. When glancing upward, I saw the large yellow sign informing me that there was not only a stop sign forthcoming but a tee in the road as well. Of course, I knew this intersection was ahead, but I didn't know it was coming up so soon.

I veered to the right while slamming my brakes. I missed plowing into the stop sign and began traveling sideways across the road. The car went airborne and landed with a crushing thud, parallel to, but very much in the ditch across the east/west road. Since seat belts were still in Ralph Nader's dream, Linda ended up on top of me, shaking with astonishment. We were safe and alive. Now to see how the car fared.

My driver's side tires, the ones away from the road were both flat. The air was seeping out from between the rims and the rubber. Somehow, the weeds had lodged inside the tires. We walked to a farmhouse nearby, explained our predicament, and the kind farmer came to our rescue.

He pulled my car out of the ditch with his tractor and a chain. His sons were enjoying the spectacle of the car and the spectacle of Linda. He dragged it to his barn, scraped out the weeds and filled my tires with air. Since I didn't have tubeless tires yet, he could do this for me without a machine. I thanked him profusely, and we continued on to Spirit Lake. We only missed the first quarter of the game; we could have easily missed the rest of our lives. Had my car hit that ditch head-on, we would have both been cut in half while blowing through the windshield. This vision was not lost on her father.

The next time I drove down there, we had a private conversation about my driving record. Had I been him, it would have been the last time my car or I ever got close to his daughter again. For some reason, he let me off with a warning. I was wondering if driving was in my future and if it was, would I even have a future. Time would tell.

**Dad's beloved 1959 Desoto in better days.
Uncle Jack in foreground.**

# CHAPTER NINETEEN

# ON A WING AND A PRAYER

During my senior year in high school I met with the guidance counselor; a recently added position by the school board, probably to comply with some state guideline. He advised me to join the Army; I could then get on the GI bill for college if I made it home alive and relatively intact.

The Viet Nam War was raging as we were talking and he thought it would be a good idea for me to get in on it before it was over. Joining the army in the sixties was a sure ticket to a miserable war no one wanted to talk about. Any war is hell, but this one was particularly nasty and hotly contested back home.

These newest vets didn't come back to a hero's welcome but as an ugly reminder of America's first losing effort. The war spawned a younger generation of non-conformity and distrust of the older generation; the greatest generation who had won their war.

These WWII veterans had brought back a victory to cheering crowds and ticker tape parades. The newest war only brought campus unrest and massive protest rallies from sea to shining sea. Television made it possible to bring all this mess into our living rooms every night, making celebrities out of those telling the awful and depressing story.

Unbelievably, the counselor was paid to give advice like this. His office was no bigger than a broom closet complete with a tiny desk and a brochure rack.

I'd seen him for four years scurrying around the halls trying to look busy shuffling his papers. I wondered how he could keep that up for the entire day, all week, month after month, for the whole year and not go nutty. Maybe he did and his army advice was a direct result of his madness, or he figured a stutter box kid didn't have much else in life to shoot for.

To my bewilderment, he always walked at a brisk pace down the halls. He reminded me of the White Rabbit in *Alice in Wonderland*. Why was he in a hurry? He didn't teach a class that I was aware of, he had nothing to be late for, and he had only to return to his broom closet to straighten out his paper clips and brochures. He needed to slow down. I doubt he took my advice. I didn't take his either.

I chose to go to Iowa State because my brother was a senior there studying landscape architecture. My parents thought it might be a good idea to have him around to help guide me. Of course, I never saw him. I even pledged his fraternity and never saw him, which was fine with both of us.

Here I was, finally among the ivy halls of higher learning that I'd heard so much about all my life. I was walking proof that I had been mistaken all those years; stutterers still stutter, even in college.

I had no idea what to major in, but I had a year or so to figure it out. I went through a bunch of career-choice brochures when sitting in the guidance counselor's office the year before in high school. Every one of them stated something about how important excellent communicative skills would be required to succeed. I was fighting a losing battle. I didn't see any brochures on the lucrative art of miming. Besides, Marcel Marceau had it all wrapped up since the world really only needs one mime at a time.

I took an aptitude test at college my second year; sort of a career placement exam. It was quite extensive, with page after page of questions and filling in little circles with a No. 2 pencil. The test took two hours to finish, and I was looking forward to seeing the results the next week.

When I got them, I couldn't believe what I was reading, "Your aptitude level of skills point to a career in sales." A salesman! Well, hell. These test people should have been around when I tried selling my night crawlers to Bob's Bait Shop. I guess I was on my own.

The week before classes started, the freshman at Iowa State were required to attend orientation in one of the biggest halls on campus. Five minutes into the presentation, the president of the university, informed us to look at the person seated on either side of us. He stated that of the three, one would not make it to graduation day. All five thousand kids of my class were dutifully turning their collective heads one way, then the other. Everyone but me, I had a pretty good idea which of the three of my group would not be making it.

During my first quarter at Iowa State University, I had a full schedule of classes: math, chemistry, English, psychology, and physical education. I dropped the math class and got poor grades on the others except my A in Phys.Ed. I didn't know how to study in the big leagues. No one cared a lick about my making the grade as there were no concerned teachers to hold my hand. I had to learn to study next term, on my own, or I was out of the fraternity, or even school. Buckling down finally, I did it the old fashioned way; I earned it.

I received a B in the math class I had dropped during the first term. This carried me just over the line academically to becoming eligible for active membership in Sigma Phi Epsilon as I was still only pledged to become one. Hell Week started on a Sunday night in late April. Of course, it was called Hell Week for a darn good reason.

All during that week, the pledges were made to strip down and wear gunny sacks whenever we were in the fraternity house. We were required to return for lunch every day and eat our food all dumped into a large jar. Hot dogs, mustard, ketchup, milk, and applesauce all mixed up together. This was by far the hardest part. Some even vomited their lunch back in the jars and were made to give it another go.

We stayed up all night to shine shoes, clean the fraternity house, and wax down our huge dining room table. It was oval-shaped and made from an old maple floor that had been salvaged from a fire. It seated forty of us. We were expected to do all this night work and still attend our classes without falling asleep in them. The active members, or actives, would have spies to make sure we didn't. If we got caught sleeping, we were automatically rejected from membership consideration.

We were all given an animal name to use during the week. Mine was "The Loon" (as in "crazy as a ..."). When my new name was announced, there was great laughter and commotion. The Loon ended up being my name for the next three years. I never heard my first name used again by any of those guys, ever, even today. Far as I know, mine was the only one that stuck.

On Friday, the actives lined us all up in the basement to reveal who did and didn't make it through. The president solemnly announced that unfortunately one of us had been caught sleeping in class and would be asked to pack up and leave. They had made arrangements with other fraternities to house all the rejects in a place off campus for the remainder of the year.

He said the slacker should be honest and man enough to admit his transgressions and step forward. Of course, all of us had been sleeping in class, but no one wanted to throw it all away if someone else might take the rap. We all stood there silently.

Finally, Wayne Beatty, a huge varsity wrestler, stepped forward. This was Iowa State wrestling I'm talking about here. They were national champs during those years. Wayne was a teammate with Dan Gable, the famed Olympic gold medal winner in 1972.

Anyway, due to Wayne's enormous size, he was probably betting on the assumption that no one had the courage to remove him from the room. He would have been correct with that assumption, but thankfully, no one had to. At that moment, all the members grabbed and congratulated us with a loud, joyous roar. In an instant, these mean-spirited actives became our equals and brothers. It was quite a day.

During the summers, I'd return to Okoboji and work for a grocery store. This was the same one adjacent to the Marion Hotel where the gopher had sunk his little yellow teeth into my thumb all those years before. I changed employment plans the summer between my sophomore and junior years.

Dave, a fellow I knew from high school and my parents' church, which I had attended all my growing up years, talked me into selling dictionaries door to door. He had made five thousand dollars the summer before, and he knew I could, too. Dave was aware of my speech problem, and I was curious he never brought it up. Even so, off I went to spend a week in Nashville to learn how to sell books. I'd receive my territory destination at the end of the training.

In Nashville, there were thousands of young men lined up getting their materials. This was a big deal for everyone there. We were to learn the preferred sales pitch by heart and be able to present it at the end of the week to our sponsors. I watched as guys younger than I rattled that stuff off with great ease. I knew I could never do what I heard those guys do. Even if I could talk, memorizing such a long sales pitch seemed out of the question.

I wished I had never committed to Dave. My parents were wondering how I would do. I'm sure my Dad had faint hopes that this might be the big step that would guide me in the right direction to success. Even though it was way out of my comfort zone, I didn't want to disappoint him. I was going to have to give it a shot.

By the time the end of the week rolled around, I was sitting in front of Dave totally unprepared to give him my pitch. I had already decided not to tackle the prepared one, assuring him that my friendly manner would get me in the doors, and my smile would take care of the rest. He assured me it wouldn't and that I should get busy and learn it as quickly as possible.

Knowing he might be right, I also knew that memorizing a long pitch would not be happening, especially one that would be impossible for me to say. What in the world was I doing here? I was missing Okoboji but going to Wilkes-Barre, Pennsylvania to sell dictionaries. Land 'o Goshen.

They drilled into us in Nashville that if we weren't out knocking on that first door by eight o'clock in the morning, sharp, on Monday, we had a fifty percent chance of failing. I was knocking on my first door on Monday at eight in the morning. Thankfully, no one was home. I sighed in relief and continued to the next house.

We were also instructed in Nashville if a woman was working in the garden or hanging her clothes out to dry that we should put down our books and offer to help her in some way. We were to reach into her basket of wet clothes, hang whatever we picked up, then start the book selling process.

My next customer was doing just that; hanging up her wash. I put down my books on the picnic table, said hi, and reached into the basket only to pull up a bra. She asked what I was doing.

"I'm j-j-just t-t-trying to help, Ma'am."

"Please get off my property or I'll call the cops," she said.

"S-S-Sorry," I apologized, as I grabbed my two books and left. What was I doing here?

It went downhill from there as if that were possible. I was wondering how I ever thought I could be a door-to-door salesman. I used to watch vacuum salesmen walk around my neighborhood when I was a kid.

They'd hide their demo behind a tree before knocking on the door, and I'd feel sorry for them when they were rejected. I imagined then how terrible a job like that must be. I was beginning to find out, first hand.

---

Years later I had a Kirby salesman knock on my door, so I got to experience their frustrations up close. I'd seen him and several others jump out of a van used to canvass the neighborhood. He came with a six pack of Coke, which would be mine if I let him in the door. While he was selling me on the dizzying array of attachments, he vacuumed the carpets, beds, and air vents and mothballed the closets. He must have had twenty round white demo filters scattered around showing me how dirty the house was.

An hour and a half later, when he told me the whole package could be mine for only $500, I just looked at him. I wasn't sure what he thought I was going to do. Finding a young man home in the morning in the middle of the week should be a pretty good indicator that a $500 vacuum may not be too high on his priority list. I told him, sorry, but thanks for the Coke. I almost asked him if it came with ice, but I didn't. He left that big pile of dirty filters in the middle of the room and slammed the door. He was not a happy vacuum cleaner salesman.

---

So anyway, here I was, far from home in Pennsylvania, trying to sell my first book. I was so alone, broke and miserable. This growing up business was going to be tough.

I went out the second day, but not for long. I found myself talking to strangers that had no desire to speak with me. I discovered that a sales pitch is all a salesman has to fall back on. I was not their friend; they didn't want to shoot the breeze with me about dictionaries. I had nothing to offer them, and I was wasting their time.

I called Dave and told him I had decided to pack up and go home. He tried to talk me out of it, but I argued this was just not going to work for me. I gathered my shirt and tie and drove back to Iowa. My job at the grocery store wasn't available, but I found another one making a small-scale model for the City of Winona, Minnesota. I made it back to Okoboji on the weekends.

Life was getting more serious all the time. I knew I had given up the book-selling job without giving it a real shot. I also knew I was going to have to confront this curse of disfluency if I was ever going to amount to a hill of beans.

My junior year, as usual, I went home for Christmas break. My sister, Marcia, who was also attending Iowa State, accompanied me. My two youngest sisters, Lisa and Leslie, who were born when I was in my early teen years, were always first to greet me at the door. Big hugs and throwing them into the air was a way to forget my troubles. They would always love me no matter what.

After my auto accidents that fateful week when I was sixteen, Lisa would come up to me when she saw me staring out the window looking into the cold gray sky. While listening to the Ray Conniff Singers on Dad's stereo, she'd touch my face with her little hand. She knew I was hurting and wanted to take away all my pain.

Fortunately, my two youngest sisters got to experience a father with a little more time and a bit more money. I was happy for them to get to know him in a different way than I had. His edges had smoothed a little. Debbie, the last of the first four siblings, was growing into a beautiful young lady. Unfortunately, she was often at odds with Dad. Deb ended up leaving home at eighteen and never looked back. She did return to assist Dad twenty years later while Mom was dying of pancreatic cancer. We all appreciated her genuine loving care.

During this particular Christmas break, Mike and his wife were home on leave from the Army serving in Manhattan, Kansas. He had fortunately secured a desk job and avoided Viet Nam. We were all thankful for that. My Mom's folks from Washington State were there as well. It was a joyous occasion for my parents, and everyone was having a delightful reunion.

After dinner, I was describing my workout schedule at the gymnasium at the school. I was living near the place, and it became a part of my routine due to its proximity. I was bragging I could do one hundred and fifty push-ups in one session, which I could. I'd never been in this good of shape before, and it was fun showing them my biceps. My two little sisters kept asking me to flex for them.

Mike had always been the bigger kid, mainly because he was older, but now he was just bigger. I was taller, but not as barrel-chested as he was. He mentioned that he'd never lost to me in an arm wrestling contest, and being in the army now, he certainly wouldn't tonight.

Considering that a challenge, we set up the table and began. I was confident he was going down. I was thrashing all my friends in school with little effort, and with an audience like we had tonight, I wouldn't be giving up.

Our eyes locked onto each other's as we took our places at the make-shift table. Then gripping hands and adjusting our elbows to help gain any advantage over the other, we began. Our knuckles turned white, our mouths contorted, and our breathing controlled; everyone was rooting for me to finally win. As we got into it, he was surprised by my newly acquired strength, but he had Army pride on his side. I was beginning to sense a bit of frustration on Mike's part, a bit of resignation. I was going to win. Then it happened. Mother of Pearl!

My humerus bone, the elbow to shoulder bone, snapped with a sickening sound heard by everyone. I screamed a bad word due to the shock and pain. It was as if someone had slammed me with a baseball bat at full swing. My arm fell to my side. When I tried to move it, I could feel the two broken parts rubbing against each other. Everyone was in total disbelief. It's not every day one gets to witness such a horrific event.

They rushed me to the hospital, but due to my recent meal, I had to wait until the next morning to have it set. Mike said when he dropped by later that night to see how I was doing, I cussed him for breaking my arm. I was undoubtedly screwy with drugs and have no recollection of him ever coming by. I'm still not sure he believes me. I guess my anger was pretty convincing.

Back at school, I had to drop all my design courses because I couldn't draw with my arm in a cast, so I fell behind in my degree progression. I now lacked in hours, and my student deferment was in jeopardy. The draft board jumped all over this opportunity like a cat on a jaybird.

I got the call to take the draft physical that spring. Interestingly enough, my knee had been doing a couple of strange things just prior to going down to Camp Dodge in Des Moines to comply with their wishes. My knee malady was nothing I had caused nor even wanted;

it just happened out of the blue. If I were to bump my knee against anything, it would burn like fire for a couple of minutes. Later I could stand in such a way that a soft tissue knob would protrude out.

I went to the base infirmary with a fraternity brother of mine, Ozzy, who had also fallen behind in his school hours. After the doctor had examined my knee, he gave me a 1-Y deferment. This would keep me out of the draft for six months, then I would be examined again to see if conditions had changed. After the six months and reexamination, they gave me a 4-F, which was a permanent deferment. I was not going to Viet Nam. However, Ozzy did. Thankfully, he made it back.

Over the next few years, I finally put in the hours it would take to earn my Bachelors of Science. Although it was what some called a working degree as opposed to so many who majored in psychology, history, or sociology, I was still lost in what I was supposed to do with it.

I sent some of my renderings (drawings) to the Indianapolis Department of Parks and Recreation, and they asked me to fly out for an interview, expenses paid. I was there by noon and was expected to spend the rest of the day getting to know them and become familiar with my potential work duties. I was to then leave the next day. The job started out at eleven thousand per year.

They were pleasent people, but I had nothing of value to say or nothing I could say without difficulty. I'd wander around each workstation trying my best to figure out what everyone was doing with their time. To me, it didn't look like they were doing much of anything. After a couple of hours, the head of the department called the airline to see if an afternoon flight was available for my trip home. They couldn't get me to the airport fast enough. One would have thought stuttering was an air-born disease.

So went my first interview. It turned out about as well as I had always expected it would. This happened twice, both, in Indianapolis. The last interview was with a large coal company headquartered there, with the same result. My drawing skills were working well enough to get me in the doors, but my communicative skills were killing me in the real world. Those high school brochures warning me about this were becoming a reality.

After graduation, I came home to Okoboji for what I thought was going to be the last time in a long while. My plans were taking me out West in an attempt to make something of myself, leaving behind all the people I knew and loved. Fear and low self-esteem had set in. Playtime was over, and my built-in student excuse I used so frequently to explain my dire circumstances of pauperism had now officially expired.

The day before my departure to the golden west, I took out the boat alone and drove around the lake, already missing it. Not wanting to leave, I was almost nauseous thinking about what may lie ahead. Leaving the relative safety of the place and the people I'd known all my life was weighing heavily on my mind.

These folks accepted me and my troubles; home is like that. What was it going to be like to look for work among strangers who might not be as understanding as I struggled to introduce myself? What employer would want that kind of problem on a daily basis?

I had acquired a Landscape Architecture degree, but had no practical experience and lacked the verbal skills to convince any potential employer to the contrary. It was embarrassing that I knew so little about my chosen field. Maybe every new graduate had these same doubts, but mine were magnified. Whatever was about to unfold had to be quick, because all I possessed was a hundred dollars and an old '64 Chevy that used more oil than gas. At least in this car, I was finally checking the dipstick. My despair and gut-wrenching fear of the foreboding future had never been this dramatic before, not even in Pennsylvania.

I felt terribly alone, but I knew I wasn't alone. Two weeks before my graduation, that prayer, offered when I was seven years old under the elm trees, had been answered. I would need this precious new knowledge to lead me onward.

Out on the lake, the sun was beginning to set beyond the shoreline of crowded oaks, the warm late May air was blowing through my hair as I skimmed silently over the glassy surface of the water. With the haunting smells of Okoboji adding to my vivid memories of this place, I was contemplating what the rest of my life had in store for me. I had to put away childish things; it was time to get busy learning to be an adult.

I brought the boat into the hoist and put her up. Looking now at the setting sun over my beloved lake, I gave her a final salute, "Goodbye, Okoboji. Thanks for always being there." I turned around and didn't look back.

**Spring of my final year at Iowa State University in 1972.**

# CHAPTER TWENTY

# FAITH IN EVERY FOOTSTEP

After arriving at my destination in the West, I started one of the only jobs I had any current experience with, janitorial work. In college, I worked part-time at the Iowa Highway Commission as a janitor/night watchman, so I naturally drifted toward the familiar. I worked the graveyard shift at a federal aviation flight controller building.

The controllers worked in one large room filled with radar screens, keeping track of all the flights in the western skies. Emptying the waste baskets was part of my duty, and I was embarrassed to have to ask them to move their feet. When I applied for the job, I told the owner of the janitorial service that I knew how to operate a floor polisher. I lied. I finally got my chance to run the machine about two weeks later.

These beastly contraptions immediately know who's in charge. It's a lot like riding a horse. If the animal senses the rider doesn't know what he's doing, he takes over from there. This powerful spinning machine dragged me around that long, wide hallway slamming me into one wall, then the other. When I reached the end of the building, I looked back at my finished product. I had ruined, what was before, an absolutely excellent floor shine. The next night, it took my boss man two hours to correct my mistakes, and I was canned. It was the only time I had ever been fired. I didn't mind so much; the night shift was a killer.

Looking on the wall at the unemployment office, I found an advertisement for a mobile home setup man. It paid two dollars and twenty-five cents an hour, fifteen cents more than the janitor job paid.

I knew nothing about mobile homes or any kind of tools that may be required to set them up. I had to be willing to travel out of town. I welcomed that and the opportunity to learn to work with tools. The only previous experience I had with using tools was losing all of Dad's collection when I was a kid.

It was summer, and I loved working outdoors. My new boss' name was Ray Wheeler. He ran a one-horse operation and was a long-time trailer setup man. Not surprisingly, he also lived in a trailer with his wife. His trailer was a single-wide, his wife, unfortunately, wasn't. Ray was bucktoothed with receding gums. He was thin, always wore a straw cowboy hat, and was a Dodge truck man through and through. A 7mm deer rifle with a scope always hung in the back window. I kidded him about his ugly Dodge. They were, by far, the ugliest vehicles on the road in the late sixties, except for any French car ever made.

Ray taught me how to thread galvanized pipe and install the water lines to the homes. I learned to attach roof ridge caps on double-wide trailers, level the homes, install gas lines and drop the front tongues to store them under the structures. There was an array of interior work to do as well, but Ray did most of that. I was becoming quite handy with tools and enjoyed the steady work.

After a whole summer of paychecks, I was ready to rid myself of my '64 Belair Chevy and buy my first sports car. The classifieds led me to check out two convertibles, a '59 Mercedes 190 SL with an $1800 asking price, and an $1100 '68 MGB. The Mercedes had a straight six-cylinder engine and a huge steering wheel which didn't quite fit my taller frame, so I opted for the smaller, but surprisingly more comfortable MGB. Bad move; the Mercedes today in modest condition goes for around $35,000.

I paid cash for the MG on a Friday night and drove the faded yellow dream car to my boarding house. The next day was a beautiful crisp fall day with an azure sky; just the kind of day to take my first ride up the mountain with the manual ragtop folded down. My head was spinning with joy, excitement, and pride. MG's ride low with the floor gearshift mounted higher than the driver's lap making for a cozy fit. It was truly a foreign sports car, and I was dazzled by it. Once more in my life, I was living large.

I headed up the canyon road with the fresh cool autumn air in my hair and lungs; the smooth roar of the Leland engine rumbling in my ears. Nearing the top of the mountain pass, I zoomed by all the shimmering golden-yellow quaking aspens and tall pines as I reached the turnaround point at a little Swedish-looking bunch of shops. I parked the car and admired it yet again against the new backdrop. After walking around the shops for five minutes as if I had something there to buy, I quickly hopped back into the car looking forward to the exhilarating drive down to the valley.

Everything was going as perfect as I'd hoped it would until I spotted a fallen rock in the middle of my driving lane. I was going too fast to stop and didn't think swerving could avoid it, so I decided to straddle it. Forgetting for an instant that this was not the Chevy Belair, I rolled over the football-sized obstacle thinking the car had more than enough clearance. At that moment, a loud crunching crumbling sound came from underneath my floorboard. The oil level gauge needle dropped immediately to zero.

Parked on the side of the road, I looked back at what might have been left behind; nothing but all my oil. I had just ruined my dream car on the first drive. The oil pan had a big hole in it and the oil pump had broken in half. Man-oh-man, what to do now?

I hitched a ride back and convinced a roommate to tow me home. After a week of fretting over what to do about it, my next door neighbor just happened to have an MGB mechanic's manual that his son had left behind. Knowing nothing about engines, I began to read about the oil pan. Only fifteen bolts secured the pan to the block, and three more bolts held the oil pump to the engine. All I would need is a new pump and its corresponding gasket, a pan gasket, and some gasket sealer. I could beat the pan back into shape and have someone weld the hole shut. I had nothing to lose. It's times like this that young men are forced to learn things they may have thought were beyond their capability.

The British manual pointed out that I would also need a "spanner" to complete the job. I didn't know what a spanner was, and no one else did either, not even Dad. I certainly didn't want to attack such a delicate operation as the removal of these eighteen bolts without the required spanner.

I went to the MG dealership downtown, where the front desk person told me to ask their resident Englishman, Malcolm, the head mechanic. Showing him the manual where it stated my need for a spanner, he smiled at me, reached into his toolbox, and handed me his spanner. It was a common wrench. Damn British language.

Tackling the job with cautious excitement, I decided to buy a used oil pump from a wrecking yard rather than buy a new one. They both looked the same, and I saved fifty bucks. This turned out to be a monumental mistake or a blessing, depending on which way one looks at it. After completing the task, I filled the engine with oil and started it up. The oil gauge needle shot off the zero mark and ended up almost to eighty psi. To be truthful it was only at sixty psi, but it was close enough for me. I would be driving my beautiful sports car again not knowing that twenty fewer pounds of oil pressure makes a big difference in the life of an engine.

This was in early September and by November the clicking sound was getting louder by the mile. I kept on driving it anyway, and on Thanksgiving Day, on my way to Ray's trailer house to eat turkey, the crankshaft finally froze to the main bearings. I had Ray tow it to his place, and it sat there, covered in snow, until early spring.

In late March, I was reading in a laundromat when a man, Jim Benson, around fortyish, asked me about my book. One thing led to another, and I ended up telling him the sad saga of my MG. He took an interest in me for some reason and offered me the use of his friend's heated garage complete with all his tools including an engine crane. Together Jim and I were going to tackle the unthinkable, an engine overhaul. I was leery, but again, I had nothing to lose; and I still had my manual and Jim's expertise.

After towing the car to the garage, we started unscrewing bolts at a rapid pace. We should have marked them as we removed them and placed them in bags, but at the time we thought remembering what went where would come naturally. After about an hour of taking the engine apart, I happened to remark how relieved I was that he was here to help since this was my first time tearing into one of these things. He replied it was his first time too. I looked at him with total shock and dismay.

Good heavens, what have I done? I had a garage floor covered with auto parts with no certainty they would ever be put to use again. There was nothing I could do about it now. We plowed ahead just the same.

After pulling the engine out, we went to work removing the valve cover, head, and crank case, exposing the damage. We removed all the main bearing caps and connecting rod caps and then the crankshaft. All of these engine parts were unknown to me, and I found the work most interesting. The bearings had melted onto the shaft due to lack of lubrication caused by the weak oil pump.

Jim helped me deliver the engine block and the crankshaft to an automotive shop to be honed and turned, respectively. In a couple of weeks, they informed me the parts were ready for pick-up. By then, however, Ray had run out of work and laid me off. With no money to pay the shop, the car sat in Jim's friend's garage until I was asked to move it out. That was the last time I saw Jim.

In early spring I moved into the second story of a two-bedroom apartment in a big new complex. Unlike my roommate, I didn't have a stick of furniture, so I slept on top of the rust-colored shag carpet in my room. My car sat outside, engine-less, in my parking space. Finally, I scraped enough money together from my new job to get the now shiny, clean engine block and the newly-turned crankshaft out of hock. I added them to the array of parts, bolts, nuts, gears, rods, and valves that were scattered all over my carpet in boxes. I didn't have a bed to sleep on, but I had my engine to snuggle with. Over the next few days, I saw up close how an engine works. After a while, it didn't seem strange at all to wake up in the mornings with pistons being my first vision of the day.

I painstakingly reassembled my engine back into one glorious piece. It's surprising how few tools are needed to perform the task; a few different sized wrenches, a torque wrench, and a piston ring compressor. My friends at the apartment complex couldn't believe what I'd been doing up in my room. It was now time to drop the engine back into the car.

I used a hand dolly and slowly brought my masterpiece out of my apartment and down the stairs. I was lucky the apartment management people didn't catch a drift of all this. Once at the car, I lowered the engine slowly into the compartment with the help of a borrowed lift. After attaching the transmission bell housing to the block and tightening down the motor mounts, I reattached the wiring to the best of my recollection.

There were at least twenty young adults out there cheering me on. Everyone had seen the engine in various stages of assembly in my room. I hadn't tried to hide it, and word would get around about the weird guy who sleeps with his motor. They probably thought I needed to date more. I agreed with that, but obviously, I didn't have transportation.

I inserted the key into the ignition switch, pumped the accelerator a few times; then turned over the starter motor. The engine roared to life to the delight of everyone there especially me. There were backslaps, handshakes, and "Hip Hip Hooray!" all around. I had succeeded at something absolutely foreign to me and way out of my comfort zone. I had overhauled an engine on my own. My Dad would hear about this shortly. I had graduated from my dipstick days.

All in all, I would say it was a blessing that I had bought a faulty used oil pump instead of a new one. Had I not, I wouldn't have had this great learning experience. I had morphed into a shade tree mechanic or rather a shag rug mechanic. This was something of which to be proud, and I was.

After being laid off by Ray, I worked as an architectural model maker for a year until he folded up shop. The experience got my design juices flowing again, and I figured it was time to test the waters associated with my bachelor's degree; landscape architecture. My brother Mike was working for a landscape contractor in Phoenix and invited me down to see what I might be able to find in the profession.

I moved to Phoenix in January of 1974. I lived with Mike and his wife for a few months and eventually sold a couple of landscape jobs to some homeowners in the area. I made a sale to a neighbor of Mike's who lived on his street. The client paid me the deposit in cash, and I went over to my brother's and threw the $900 into the air to celebrate. It was my first landscape sales attempt.

One day Mike suggested we start a business together. He liked the idea of us working for ourselves and I agreed. He certainly was much more familiar with desert plant materials than I was and he may have needed my example to push him out of the employee safety nest into the world of self-employment. We were a good match. We acquired a contractor's license, insurance, some signage, some hand tools, and two wheelbarrows. We also bought a new one-ton pickup for $5200 on time payments.

We were officially in business. Our first six months were slim pickings, having only smaller jobs from some of Mike's friends. I was back knocking on doors again, but this time, I wasn't selling books.

We kept it going, but just enough to get by. I remember when we had our first back-to-back jobs. For the first time we didn't have to store our tools in his garage after finishing up on a project; instead, we took them over to the next one. It was a great feeling. We ran this company for over twenty years.

After a while, we were too busy for both of us to work at the job site all day and then draw plans to sell at night, so we divided our responsibilities. He took over the drawing and selling while I ran the crews. It was still difficult for me to pronounce the names of the plant materials and to generally describe what the homeowners were considering. Landscape designs are conceptual and need to be effectively explained to be sold. I couldn't do it without great difficulty. I'd usually end up with no contract and a terrific migraine headache. No one in the real world is going to lay down that kind of cash because they felt sorry for me.

One day, before leaving the house for work, I was reading a story in the newspaper about Sen. John Glenn's wife, Annie. The movie, *The Right Stuff*, was all the rage at the time, and some journalist had picked up on Annie Glenn, whose character was a part of the movie. Her husband John was the first American to orbit the earth. He circled the globe three times in February of 1962 and was given a ticker-tape parade in Manhattan, not unlike Charles Lindbergh received for his trans-Atlantic flight to Paris.

The article mentioned how Annie had struggled all her life with the curse of being a stutterer. The story stated that she had attended a speech therapy course at Hollins College in Roanoke, Virginia and that she was now speaking at various events. I called the school that very minute and set up my three-week therapy course with them. I left two weeks later. I was thirty years old; it was time to fix this damned thing.

In the past, I'd always avoided anyone who had a speech defect. Most stutterers feel the same way. It's just too painful to witness. When our class arrived at the appointed location, we all got to meet our fellow stutterers for the first time. There were twenty of us clucking and spitting away, attempting to convince anyone who would listen that we didn't really need to be there. What a video that would've made.

Heavens to Betsy! I thought I had troubles; this was a real eye opener. It's strange that everyone there had their own unique form of stutter or at least their own unique way of attempting to mask it. I wouldn't have traded my brand of stuttering for anyone of theirs, and I'm sure they felt the same way. Even though we hated our own speech pattern, it was still *our* speech pattern; we found everyone else's much more disturbing. Except for maybe two of them; those two would've happily switched with anyone.

We were filmed individually before our three-week session started. We could all hear what was going on in the filming room down the hall. I was looking at the floor, shaking my head while some of the strangest sounds came forth from down the hallway. It was truly disturbing.

One of the worst stutterer's utterances resembled a flat tire flapping on the roadway. This person had the worst speech blocks I could ever imagine. Instead of just stopping and taking a deep breath, the creature continued to plow on through to the next word blockage. There was seemingly no end to it. All of us fellow stutterers in the room looked at each other and winced.

When the poor unfortunate student responsible for creating that sound came into our waiting room, my jaw and everyone else's dropped. She was a darling sixteen-year-old girl with a face like Elizabeth Taylor's; almond-shaped blue eyes and all. Even I couldn't imagine what life for her must have been like up until now with that crippling stammer. The baffling form of speech that was produced from her beautiful face was almost inhuman. This was why she hadn't tried to talk to anyone when we first met. There's a point in time when maybe learning sign language would have been a viable option.

There was one other fellow who was not as disturbing to listen to as Miss Elizabeth, but he was certainly in the running. He had just finished dental school, and his father was back in Chicago busily opening a new office so his son could start his business. The new dentist simply had to rid himself of this one pesky little problem before he was off to dental practice heaven; presently, he could not utter any words at all.

He tried gallantly, but we had to walk away from him the same way we had had people walk away from us all our lives. There was no point in standing there waiting for him to say something; he wasn't going to get it out before sundown. Everyone there wondered how, in the name of Moses, he graduated dental school; or for that matter, grade school? What a curse. We all hoped this program had a magic answer. Marbles in the mouth weren't going to do it, not in this place.

One night the dentist came over to my room to watch the Phoenix Suns in a playoff game. After a basket was made by Kevin Johnson, I yelled, "Great shot!"

From behind me, where he was seated, I heard a sound, "Sh-sh-sh-sh-sh-sh-sh-sh-sh-sh-sh-sh ..." This went on for well over an entire minute. He even took a couple of breaths between these utterances to load up again only to continue on with this attempt at speech. Over a minute of this is an eternity in stutter-world. I didn't turn around to acknowledge his addressing me; it was too uncomfortable. I kept watching the game, pretending to not hear him. I couldn't help but wonder how many times this exact scenario may have occurred in my lifetime. I understood why Dad wouldn't want to stay in the same room with me whenever I was having difficulty communicating with him.

Finally, he came out with, "... sh-sh-sh-sure was."

He was only trying to say two little words, "sure was." How on earth was this guy ever going to convince his patients that they were about to experience a little pressure from the needle hidden behind his leg?

On that first Monday, the rules were laid out for us to strictly follow. We were each issued a stopwatch to carry around with us whenever we were in class from eight in the morning until five in the afternoon. (I still have mine.) They taught us how to speak in two-second syllables, keeping our eyes on the moving dial. During the entire first week, we were to only speak according to this rule. If we got off target, the therapist would interrupt us and point to our stopwatch. If the building happened to be burning and we were attempting to yell FIRE!, they would've pointed to our stopwatch and ignored us.

As one can easily imagine, this restriction was most disturbing and murderous to get used to. Two seconds per syllable was annoying and seemingly ridiculous. It's as if the speech process was now bogged down in the mud. The following is an example of how this would sound to the listener using the sentence, "Hello, my name is Doug."

While looking at the stopwatch, I would begin, "Heeeellla loooowa, myeeeya naaaama izzzah Duuuuga." Each syllable would be two full seconds to complete.

They paired us off to start things going. There was some rebellion among the students, and we attempted to buck the system from the get-go. The therapists would have none of it; it was their way or the highway. We were all thinking we had something of importance to relay to our listening partner, forgetting that absolutely none of that mattered. It wasn't *what* we were saying that was important, but rather *how* we were saying it. It's the only reason we were there having spent the $3500 tuition fees for the privilege. As the first day went on, frustrations and tempers flared and old-speak returned.

The most astonishing result emerged when speaking in the two-second syllable mode; all stuttering ceased, even Miss Elizabeth's. We could enjoy her real voice for the first time.

The problem with speaking like this, of course, is that no listener in the real world would hang around long enough to hear what you had to say.

We spent most of our eight hours a day in our own little cubicles going over speech exercises; actually breaking down the individual sounds of speech. The goal was to master a part of speech using soft onsets instead of hard onsets. An onset is the instant the vocal chords begin to vibrate. To say it another way, the activation of the vocal chords is the onset of speech. Most stutterers don't have a problem when whispering because vocal chords aren't coming into play; they're not vibrating to give real speech sounds.

We had a small box sitting on our tiny desk with a microphone attached to it. We'd say various words from the manual into the microphone, hoping the light wouldn't glow indicating we had blown the soft onset parameter. We'd have to keep at it until we managed to get through the day's exercises without the light blinking. It was miserable work.

The next week we were allowed to speak in one-second syllables. This doubled the speed of the conversation, and stuttering continued to be absent when applying this technique, but it was still annoying to be either the speaker or the listener.

Whenever someone wanted to actually express his feelings about something, tell a story, or just vent his frustrations concerning this new crazy way of speaking into a stopwatch, his old speech pattern would emerge. It happened all the time and was fascinating to observe. The ironic part was, if he had used the stopwatch technique, it would have taken him far less time to tell the story or vent his frustrations. His normal way of speaking was much slower and way more disturbing than what we were now required to do.

The first half of the third week we spoke in half-second syllables. As long as we remained on target, we weren't experiencing any disfluency. The last half of the week we were making calls from our individual booths to local stores asking for things like gutters or hair blowers. We were off the clock now, and we made a Thursday afternoon trip to the mall to test our new abilities on real live people.

Most of the twenty students benefitted from the three-week intensive training, but some didn't put in the work. A fifteen-year old boy didn't think it was critical enough to bear down and do the exercises in his cubicle all day. He had his Walkman attached to his headset instead of his black box like everyone else. He left the program exactly the same as when he came in. He would undoubtedly return someday on his own instead of at his parents' insistance.

As one can imagine, being cooped up like that for three weeks, tempers would flare at times between the different personalities. After all, we may have been comrades-in-arms, suffering from the same malady, but we weren't friends. Whenever words were exchanged, they were usually done in the old language-speak that the students brought to this place, which only tended to make the already heated situation worse. I stayed out of all that nonsense.

Miss Elizabeth did a terrific job. Her father came to bring her home and began crying when he heard how she had blossomed. The dentist improved, but probably not enough to pull off a successful practice. Hopefully, he went back to Hollins for a second shot at it.

Those of us who were beginning to master the technique of producing the soft onsets were hopeful it would last; that day by day, this miracle wouldn't chip away and fall apart.

When I returned home, I was almost 100% fluent. Most folks walking around are about 93%. My family and friends were hanging on every word I spoke. I concentrated on all my new found techniques of generating the softer onset. All of the speech graduates were to practice our exercises every day in normal speaking situations as well as alone at home using our manual.

Still, I was frightened it might not last, that the cure would wear off. I'd spent too many years being humiliated and rejected to think anything could permanently fix this thing. As with most everything else in life, it would depend on the drive and energy directed toward the end result.

I was always hoping for an easy cure, some magic dust from Tinkerbell to help me, not some exercise I would have to master for the rest of my life. It's almost as if having normal fluency has a price tag, and I have to ask myself if I'm willing to pay it on a daily basis. Habits are some of life's biggest stumbling blocks.

Ever the singer, I now had enough confidence to audition for musical theater. I was cast in several plays and even a few that weren't musicals. This opened an avenue of expression previously closed to me, even though I was too late to snag the Captain Von Trapp role opposite Peggy Smart in *The Sound of Music*.

Today, from time to time, I'm asked to speak in my church like everyone else. I write my talks and look forward to giving them; I'm actually chomping at the bit before I'm introduced. If I've written a good talk, I'm an entertaining speaker. I recently spoke at my Dad's funeral in Iowa. It was a twenty minute talk, but I wanted it to go on for much longer. The fear of disfluency didn't come into play. It wasn't on my mind. I knew it wouldn't be. I hope Dad was there to hear it.

Still, I have my weaker moments when I'm tired or not interested in the current conversation when some of the old speech patterns might emerge. Due to its lack of frequency or intensity, I'm not too alarmed by it. The reality that I know I can speak fluently if I focus on it, is a huge advantage over not having any confidence at all. It seems surreal after all this time and torture, but it boils down to this: I can overcome my stuttering depending on how much desire I have to do it. I possess the cure. It's just up to me to use it. Most of life's problems can be solved this way; in the end, it's up to us.

———————

Sometimes I think of that little boy back in Okoboji delivering papers, walking quietly before dawn in the snow. He's wondering how he's ever going to get through the day, let alone an entire lifetime, ordained as an outsider in a fluent world. He's not interested in this now, but maybe, just maybe, his affliction was a godsend to help make him more teachable, more humble than he might otherwise have been. He needs to realize this life was never meant to be fair, that trials and tribulations are put in our pathway to make us stronger. The little paperboy needs to keep plowing through his life, gleaning the goodness out of it.

He will eventually be aware that being born into his family was a fortuitous event. Here he will be nurtured and cared for until he's ready to take on the world. There will be people surrounding him throughout his life to give guidance, encouragement, and support.

He doesn't know it yet, but he has the blessing of being an American, living in a miraculous country protected not only by two great oceans but also by a Constitution inspired by the very God of this earth; a gift shared by relatively few in this world.

This, however, will require time, perseverance, hope, and above all, faith in every footstep. In the meantime, keep delivering those papers, young man. Don't forget, two rolls and a Pepsi are just around the corner.

# Th-Thee-Th-Thee-Th-Thee
# That's all Folks!

**Doug lives in Arizona with his wife, Janice.**

okoboji.kidd@gmail.com

Made in the USA
Middletown, DE
06 October 2020

21203308R00116